# What Life Was Like ®

## IN THE LAND OF THE DRAGON

### Imperial China
### AD 960 ~ 1368

# What Life Was Like

## IN THE LAND OF THE DRAGON

Imperial China
AD 960 ~ 1368

BY THE EDITORS OF TIME-LIFE BOOKS, ALEXANDRIA, VIRGINIA

# CONTENTS

# In the Land of the Dragon

# MASTERS OF THE MIDDLE KINGDOM

More than 100 years before the Romans ruled the Mediterranean, the Chinese forged a mighty empire they called the Middle Kingdom—the heart of the civilized world, they believed, encompassing everything under heaven that was worth having. In this realm, as one Chinese sage put it, "Nature thrives luxuriantly, arts and crafts are richly developed, ruler and people occupy their proper places, and morality and justice support each other."

But the Middle Kingdom was also a place of endless contrasts and conflict. From the beginning, those who hammered the empire together were challenged by forces who resented imperial domination or coveted power themselves. By the time a shrewd young general named Zhao Kuangyin founded the Song dynasty in the year 960, China's 1,200-year-old empire had endured several prolonged intervals of disunion and strife like the one that followed the collapse of the Tang dynasty in 906. During such chaotic periods, it seemed as if the Middle Kingdom would never regain heaven's blessing.

Yet Zhao and his successors had great traditions to draw upon in their campaign to restore China to glory. They could not claim to be heirs of the Tang emperors or their royal predecessors (each successive dynasty represented a new bloodline, and some who founded dynasties even hailed from beyond China's borders). But they could and did appeal to the reverence of the Chinese people for their imperial heritage and to their longing for peace. By the end of the 10th century, through a deft combination of diplomatic inducements and military pressure, Zhao and his successor, Taizong, had succeeded in restoring to the empire most of its traditional territories.

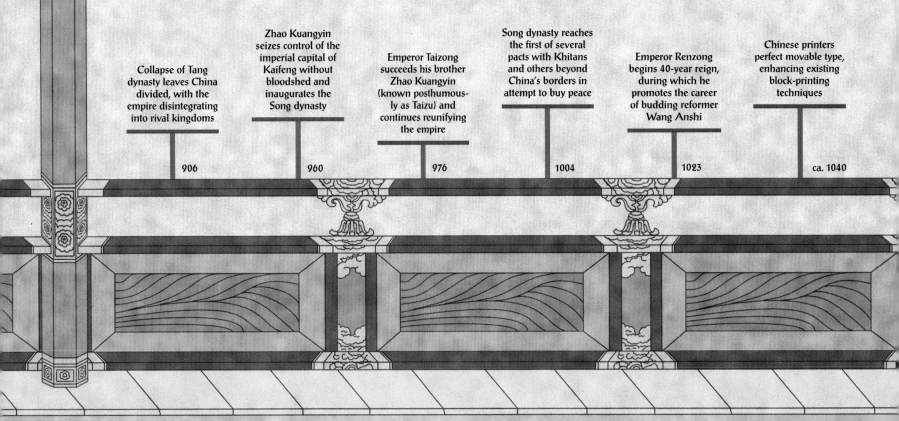

**Collapse of Tang dynasty leaves China divided, with the empire disintegrating into rival kingdoms**

**Zhao Kuangyin seizes control of the imperial capital of Kaifeng without bloodshed and inaugurates the Song dynasty**

**Emperor Taizong succeeds his brother Zhao Kuangyin (known posthumously as Taizu) and continues reunifying the empire**

**Song dynasty reaches the first of several pacts with Khitans and others beyond China's borders in attempt to buy peace**

**Emperor Renzong begins 40-year reign, during which he promotes the career of budding reformer Wang Anshi**

**Chinese printers perfect movable type, enhancing existing block-printing techniques**

906     960     976     1004     1023     ca. 1040

Stiff challenges awaited the reunified empire. Beyond its frontiers lurked powerful rivals—notably the Khitans of Manchuria, the first of several northern foes adept at mounted warfare who would bedevil the Song dynasty. Moreover, any effort by China's rulers to respond to such challenges by enlarging the army, improving roads or fortifications, or hiking taxes for defense meant greater hardship for the peasants.

How to bolster China without driving the peasants to ruin or revolt became a hot issue among the emperors' advisers—keen scholar-officials who drew inspiration from the ancient master Kongzi, known to the West as Confucius. His maxims set high moral standards for the ruling class: "Approach your duties with reverence and be trustworthy in what you say; avoid excesses in expenditure and love your fellow men; employ the labour of the common people only in the right seasons."

Among those who sought to apply the lessons of Confucius to China's pressing problems was Wang Anshi, chief councilor to Song dynasty emperor Shenzong. Beginning in 1069 Wang enacted sweeping reforms called the New Policies, aimed at strengthening the state while improving the lot of the peasants. Wang's ambitious programs drew sharp opposition both from rich landowners who selfishly resisted any effort to tax the wealthy for the good of the poor and from scholar-officials who conscientiously opposed what they saw as the reformers' attempts to meddle in the lives of the people. This great debate over the proper role of the state in promoting the public good—which would reverberate in China into modern times—so divided the imperial family and the bureaucracy that the government became virtually paralyzed. After Shenzong's death in 1085, Wang's policies were revoked, and subsequent emperors did little to address China's economic or military shortcomings.

The empire was ripe for conquest, and in 1126 fierce invaders from the north called the Jurchens, who had recently overthrown their Khitan overlords in Manchuria, swept down into

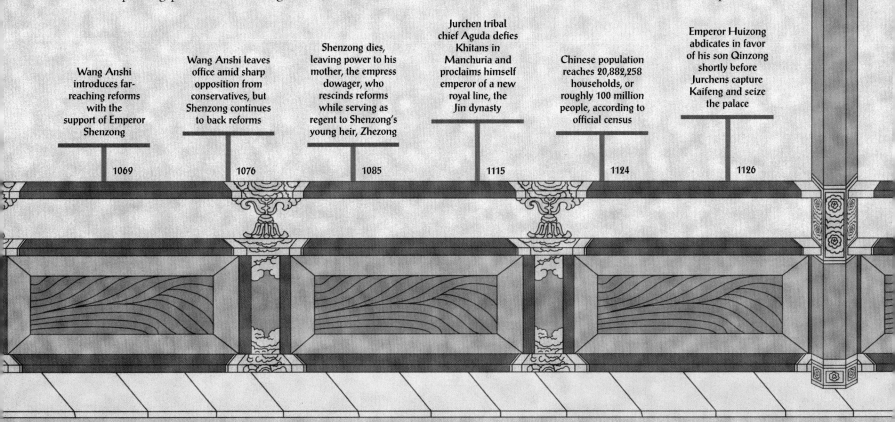

Wang Anshi introduces far-reaching reforms with the support of Emperor Shenzong

Wang Anshi leaves office amid sharp opposition from conservatives, but Shenzong continues to back reforms

Shenzong dies, leaving power to his mother, the empress dowager, who rescinds reforms while serving as regent to Shenzong's young heir, Zhezong

Jurchen tribal chief Aguda defies Khitans in Manchuria and proclaims himself emperor of a new royal line, the Jin dynasty

Chinese population reaches 20,882,258 households, or roughly 100 million people, according to official census

Emperor Huizong abdicates in favor of his son Qinzong shortly before Jurchens capture Kaifeng and seize the palace

1069          1076          1085          1115          1124          1126

China on horseback and sacked the capital of Kaifeng. Among those they seized as prisoners were the reigning Song emperor Qinzong; his spendthrift father Huizong, who had recently abdicated; and thousands of councilors, courtesans, eunuchs, physicians, fortunetellers, musicians, and serving women who had surrounded the pampered Song rulers in their palace enclave. Only a few members of the ruling family escaped—notably Huizong's ninth son, Gaozong, who fled south and rallied forces to resist the Jurchens. After several years of sharp conflict, the two sides came to terms, with the Jurchens claiming northern China and Gaozong securing control of the south.

The Southern Song, as Gaozong and his imperial successors were known, had the good fortune to retain the richest and most productive part of China. In the south lay abundant rice fields and a splendid network of rivers and canals that fostered transportation and commerce, which was further enhanced by advances in shipbuilding and other technological innovations. Gaozong's new

capital in the south, Hangzhou, was already a vibrant economic and cultural center when he arrived—thanks in part to the good work of civic officials like Wang Anshi's contemporary, Su Shi, a great poet and principled administrator. Under the Southern Song, Hangzhou grew to become the greatest city in the world, with a population of over a million and a wondrous array of shops, markets, and landscaped residences for the wealthy.

This was a time of heightened contrasts in China—between the rich and the poor, and between the pursuit of sensual pleasures and the search for spiritual fulfillment. Never had those in high positions been more comfortable, yet many still hungered for enlightenment. They sought lessons in self-denial from Buddhist priests or studied with Daoist holy men, who discouraged their followers from striving after worldly success. The masters of a new school of Confucianism challenged the complacency of the ruling class. "If you spend ten days a month preparing for the examinations," remarked Zhu Xi, a leading Neo-

Gaozong, Huizong's ninth son, having eluded capture, comes to terms with Jurchens and founds Southern Song dynasty

1141

Hangzhou officially designated the capital of Southern Song; Gaozong builds imperial palace there

1148

Chinggis Khan proclaimed ruler of Mongols and prepares for campaigns of conquest

1206

Mongols under Chinggis assail Jurchens and destroy Zhongdu, capital of the Jin dynasty in northern China

1215

Mongol forces complete conquest of northern China with help from Southern Song

1234

Khubilai Khan becomes ruler of vast Mongol Empire, including northern China, where he will establish a new capital

1260

Confucianist who took a dim view of the civil service and its exams, "you will still have twenty days to do real study." China's leaders, he feared, were ill prepared for the challenges of an uncertain future: "The cosmos changes; there is no constancy."

Change came to China with a vengeance in the 13th century in the form of the invading Mongols. Indomitable horsemen from the steppes of central Asia, they seized most of northern China under the generalship of Chinggis, or Genghis, Khan in 1215 and completed the conquest of the north in 1234. In 1260 Chinggis's ambitious grandson, Khubilai Khan, assumed control of the Mongol Empire and set his sights on the rich domain of the Southern Song, whose leadership was riven by dissension and did little to prepare for the onslaught. Song forces nonetheless put up a hard fight when the Mongols launched their climactic campaign in 1275. Hangzhou fell the following year, but die-hard loyalists held out against the invaders along the southeast coast until the Mongols crushed them in 1279.

The victorious Khubilai Khan was a ruler of some imagination and flexibility who modeled the Yuan dynasty he founded after Chinese precedents. But he shouldered enormous tasks— including the construction of a new capital at Beijing and epic campaigns against Japan and other Asian countries—and financed them with crushing taxes. Essentially still an alien in China, he trusted officials imported from abroad more than he did local administrators, and in any case, few Chinese scholar-officials were willing to serve under the Mongols.

After Khubilai's death in 1294, the Yuan dynasty declined rapidly. When floods in the 1340s destroyed part of the Grand Canal, a vital artery linking north China to the south, despised officials conscripted vast numbers of people for the laborious reconstruction, leading to the first in a string of rebellions. Finally, in 1368, the rebel leader Zhu Yuanzhang expelled the Mongols and inaugurated the Ming dynasty. Once again, the Middle Kingdom was united under heaven—and safely in Chinese hands.

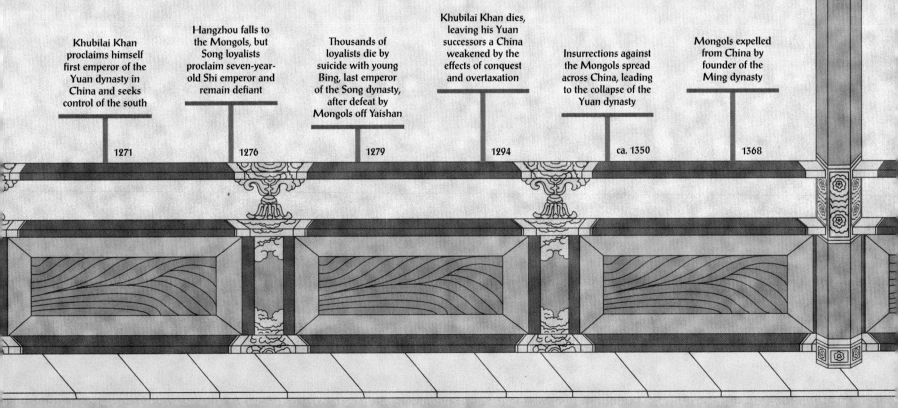

**Khubilai Khan proclaims himself first emperor of the Yuan dynasty in China and seeks control of the south**

1271

**Hangzhou falls to the Mongols, but Song loyalists proclaim seven-year-old Shi emperor and remain defiant**

1276

**Thousands of loyalists die by suicide with young Bing, last emperor of the Song dynasty, after defeat by Mongols off Yaishan**

1279

**Khubilai Khan dies, leaving his Yuan successors a China weakened by the effects of conquest and overtaxation**

1294

**Insurrections against the Mongols spread across China, leading to the collapse of the Yuan dynasty**

ca. 1350

**Mongols expelled from China by founder of the Ming dynasty**

1368

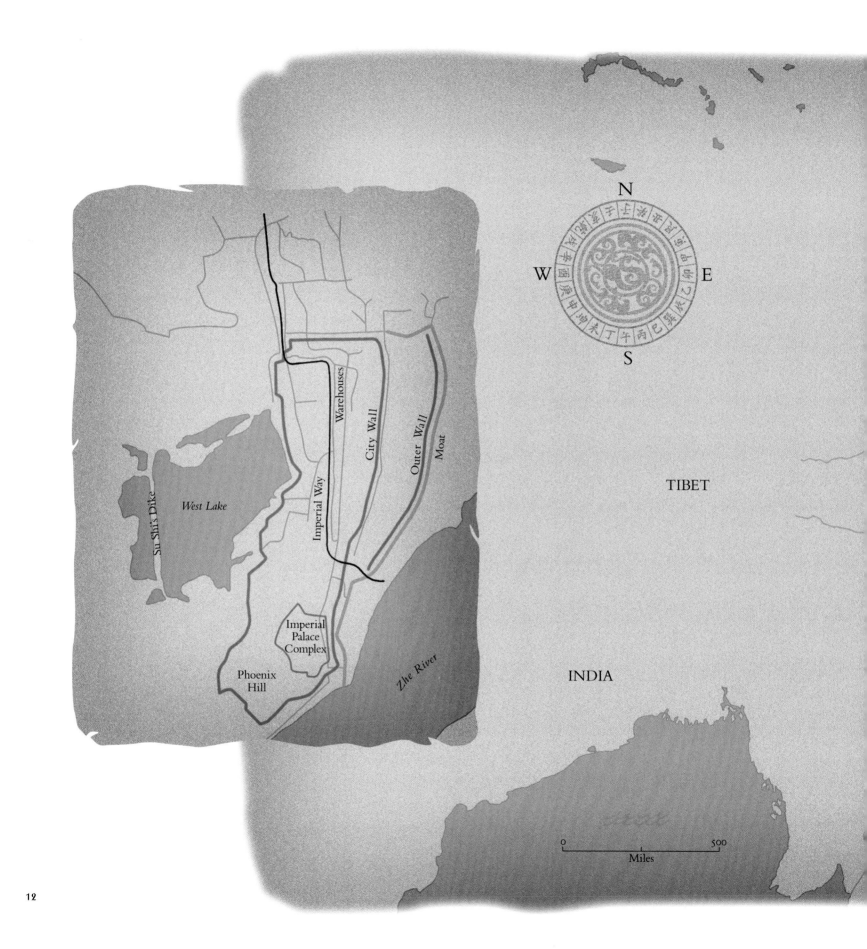

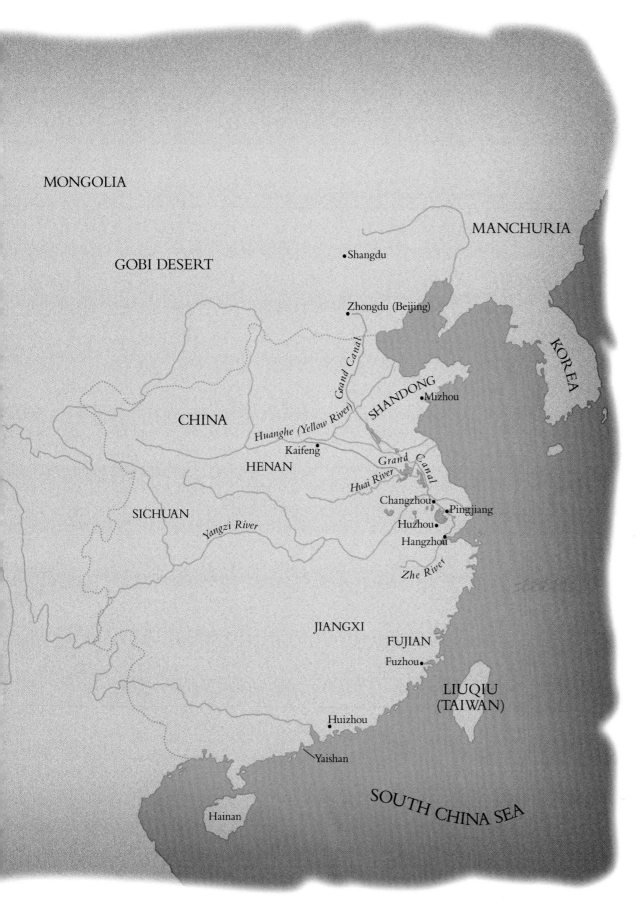

MONGOLIA

GOBI DESERT

MANCHURIA

•Shangdu

Zhongdu (Beijing)
•

CHINA

Grand Canal

KOREA

SHANDONG
•Mizhou

Huanghe (Yellow River)

Kaifeng
•

HENAN

Grand Canal

Huai River

Changzhou•
•Pingjiang

Huzhou•

Hangzhou
•

SICHUAN

Yangzi River

Zhe River

JIANGXI

FUJIAN

Fuzhou•

LIUQIU
(TAIWAN)

Huizhou
•

Yaishan

SOUTH CHINA SEA

Hainan

The first rulers of the Song dynasty restored China to greatness culturally and territorially. At its height in the 11th century, the Song empire comprised the area shown here within the dotted line—a smaller area than China would later encompass but still a vast and wealthy domain, containing some of the world's grandest cities and most fertile fields. The Song made their capital originally at Kaifeng, near the Huanghe, or Yellow River, the cradle of Chinese civilization.

After the Jurchens swept down from Manchuria in the early 12th century, the Southern Song retained the area below the Huai River. This included the prime rice-growing region extending southward from the Yangzi River basin. The teeming Southern Song capital of Hangzhou *(detail, opposite)* drew on that agricultural wealth and on the commerce that flourished on the Grand Canal and other waterways. The city—surrounded by a great wall, crisscrossed by canals *(light blue)*, and adjoined by beautiful West Lake—remained a place of astonishing variety and vitality even after it fell to the Mongols in 1276.

# CHAPTER ONE

# Guardians of the Realm

Zhao Kuangyin, the founder of the Song dynasty who seized power in the year 960, sits serenely on a throne embellished with gilded dragon heads, which symbolized his imperial might. Only the emperor and his leading officials were entitled to wear a scholar's cap with its sidepieces, or "feet," extending straight out, as shown here.

Some men were born to rule over China, and others fought their way to that pinnacle with ruthless determination, never resting until they reached their goal.

But for Zhao Kuangyin, a gifted young commander who was destined to found the Song dynasty and forge a greater China, the call to imperial glory came as a rude awakening. He was sleeping in his tent in northern China one morning in the year 959 when a group of his fellow officers rushed in at daybreak with swords drawn, roused him from bed, and forced him to don the yellow robe of Chinese royalty. In hailing Zhao as their ruler, the officers were also inducting him as leader of their mutiny against the recently installed emperor, a mere boy controlled by his mother, the empress regent, whom the rebels regarded as hostile to their interests.

The 31-year-old Zhao was a big man with broad views who hailed from a long line of cultivated and accomplished officers, and he responded to this jarring summons with the wisdom of someone twice his age. He consented to lead the rebellion, but only on his own terms. Before marching on Kaifeng—China's bustling imperial capital situated at the confluence of the Yellow River and the Grand Canal, which linked northern China to the fertile south—he demanded from his officers an oath of obedience and insisted that they harm neither the emperor himself nor his mother, nor any other imperial relative, government official, or defenseless citizen.

Resistance in the capital soon crumbled, and in 960 Zhao's forces swept into Kaifeng and deposed the boy emperor without bloodshed, thus bringing to a merciful end the troubled Zhou dynasty, whose domain encompassed only a portion of the once-mighty Chinese empire that the energetic new ruler would soon begin to reassemble. In establishing the Song dynasty, named for his ancestral home in the surrounding province of Henan, Zhao did all he could to appease his predecessors and their supporters, permitting the former ruling family to live freely in Kaifeng.

Indeed, Zhao saw less to fear from those he ousted than from the ambitious commanders who raised him to power. In launching the mutiny, those officers had willingly defied the Son of Heaven, as each successive emperor of China was reverently known. How long would they remain faithful to their new overlord? To settle the matter, Zhao invited his top commanders to a banquet in Kaifeng at the sprawling palace complex—a walled city within the city, graced with gardens, pavilions, and residences with roofs of glazed tiles housing hundreds of imperial retainers. Amid those lavish surroundings, his guests partook freely of the food and wine offered by gracious serving women. Choosing his moment, Zhao waited until his commanders were satisfied and at ease before addressing them gravely in terms that would later be set down in an official chronicle of his reign.

"I do not sleep peacefully at night," the emperor announced.

"Why?" asked one of his startled guests.

"It is not hard to understand," he replied. "Which of you does not covet my throne?"

The commanders bowed deeply and protested that none of them had such a treacherous desire. That might be, Zhao conceded, "but if one day one of you is roused at dawn, and forced to don a yellow robe, even if unwilling, how should you avoid being obliged to overthrow the Song, just as I against my will was forced to overthrow the Zhou?"

His guests hastily assured him that none of them was worthy of such a distinction. Having maneuvered his commanders into stating his case for him, Zhao now proposed to them nothing less than their withdrawal from public life.

"The life of man is short," he declared. "Happiness is to have the wealth and means to enjoy life, and then to be able to leave the same prosperity to one's descendants. If you, my officers, will renounce your military authority, retire to the provinces, and choose there the best lands and most delightful dwelling-places, there to pass the rest of your lives in pleasure and peace until you die of old age, would this not be better than to live a life of peril and uncertainty?" As further inducement, he promised to tie their families to his through marriage, so that they would forever be linked to him "in friendship and amity."

Whatever their private thoughts, the commanders could see no way of refusing the emperor's offer, which would sweep them ever so gently from the scene. The next day, citing imaginary illnesses, they all resigned and retired to homes in the country, where they duly received the rewards promised them.

The bloodless fashion in which Zhao dispensed with his worrisome commanders characterized his enlightened reign as a whole as well as the shrewd manner in which he rebuilt the fractured Chinese empire. True to his military training, he maintained a sizable army and used it to pressure some breakaway states into returning to the imperial fold. But he accomplished more through inducements than through threats. Rulers who submitted and brought their states back within the empire trusted that he would be merciful and generous toward them, as he had been toward others who yielded. He cleverly portrayed his campaign to reunify China as a golden opportunity for errant provinces to rejoin a great family. When the ruler of one southern state asked if he could retain control of his domain as the emperor's vassal,

Women prepare a sumptuous feast in the foreground of this 10th-century painting on silk, which shows an artfully landscaped residence of the sort that sheltered the imperial family and others of wealth and distinction. The airy buildings with their sloping tile roofs opened onto shaded courtyards and gardens that offered peace and seclusion, even to those in busy cities like Kaifeng.

Zhao politely refused, insisting on complete authority over that state. What crime had people there committed, he asked pointedly, that they should be "separated from the empire?"

At his death in 976, Zhao—known posthumously as Taizu, or Supreme Progenitor—was succeeded by his capable younger brother, Taizong, who continued the process of consolidating the empire. Some claimed that Taizong usurped power from Zhao's son and rightful heir. But the official story was that Zhao bequeathed power to his brother at the insistence of his mother (even the Son of Heaven had to bow to his mother). By the time Zhao fathered a male heir, he was no longer young, and his mother feared that he might die before the boy matured. As her own death approached, she reportedly urged him to appoint his brother as successor rather than the young prince.

When Zhao questioned this surprising proposal, the old woman summoned her strength and pressed her case. "Why do you suppose that you have obtained the empire?" she asked.

Zhao replied deferentially that his rise to emperor was due no doubt to the virtues of his esteemed mother and ancestors.

"Neither I nor your ancestors have anything to do with it," she insisted. "The only reason that you are on the throne today is because the late emperor was so foolish as to nominate a young child as his successor. If you are succeeded by a child, our dynasty will suffer the fate that we meted out to them."

Moved as much by his mother's unassailable logic as by his desire to honor her, Zhao acceded to her wish and left the empire in his brother's strong hands, thus perpetuating a dynasty that endured for three centuries and that presided over one of the most fruitful eras in Chinese history.

Zhao's mother was one of many forceful women who exercised great influence at the highest levels of Chinese society at a time when men claimed mastery over women—in theory, if not in practice. "Between man and woman, there is an order of superiority and inferiority," wrote one Chinese scholar influenced by Confucius—known to the Chinese as Kongzi—whose ancient teachings, stressing the obligations of respect and consideration that social inferiors and superiors owed each other, were revived and reinterpreted during the Song dynasty. Another Chinese writer warned men against allowing women to take the initiative, "Do not allow the disaster of the hen announcing the dawn."

Despite such inflexible pronouncements, men in the Song period often heeded the advice of women and deferred to them in domestic matters, including the management of the imperial household. As one authority put it, "The men are in charge of all affairs on the outside; the women manage the inside affairs." Even the most conservative Confucianists believed that men were superior only insofar as they met their obligations to their wives and others who depended on them, much as rulers had to fulfill their responsibilities to their subjects. Furthermore, the piety that every son owed to his mother in Chinese society brought women a measure of respect and elevated the emperor's mother, in particular, to a position of great authority.

Not all Song emperors were as careful in planning for the succession as the dynastic founder, Zhao. On several occasions, a dying Song emperor left the throne to a son who was too young to rule and who came under the regency of his own mother or his father's mother, if she was still alive. This regent, known as the empress dowager, was more than just a caretaker.

Empress Dowager Cao, flanked by two attendants and wearing a crown adorned with dragons and pearls, ruled as regent for the future emperor Yingzong, who was too ill to take the throne when his father died. Fond of power, Cao yielded only grudgingly to Yingzong after he recovered.

Until the young prince was considered mature to enough to rule, usually around the age of 17, the empress dowager was China's acting sovereign, although she held court at the palace from behind a screen to preserve the illusion that her role was private rather than public.

In truth, the women who occupied this lofty position were often politically adept—and some clung to power longer than they were supposed to. One remained regent until the prince under her care was 23 years old and, as her own death approached, tried to transfer the regency to another woman. That effort was blocked by imperial ministers, one of whom argued that the people of China would not take to being "mothered" any longer. Another empress dowager, named Cao, assumed the regency not because the male heir to the throne was too young but because he was too ill to perform his duties. He eventually recovered, but Cao refused to make way for him. Finally, one of her opponents shamed her by removing the screen that shielded her from view while she was holding court, forcing her to flee in disgrace and relinquish her position.

In some ways, the women who served as regent were better prepared for the intrigue and maneuvering at court than the princes they watched over. While her husband lived, an empress had to cope with any number of female rivals. She was the ruler's principal wife, but he had many more to choose from. At one point in the distant past, it was said, the emperor was theoretically entitled to 121 female consorts of various grades, but Song rulers made do with about 10 women on average. The wives were organized in an elaborate hierarchy, and many a Song empress faced stiff competition from secondary wives who might be raised to the top rank if they made themselves especially pleasing to the emperor by virtue of their charms or by providing him with healthy male heirs. An empress who prevailed in such circumstances and lived to become regent to the emperor's youthful successor was a woman to be reckoned with.

There was more to palace politics than rivalries between the wives. Among those who figured prominently in disputes at court were eunuchs, singled out for that role as boys and castrated so that they might safely reside among the palace women without seducing them. Eunuchs themselves coveted power and maneuvered for advantage, however. Long before the founding of the Song dynasty, palace eunuchs had grappled their way to high positions as generals and imperial councilors. Distressed by that trend, in the year 835 civil officials had joined with the reigning emperor in an effort to purge such potent eunuchs from the administration, but the eunuchs alertly foiled that scheme and struck back with a vengeance. Hundreds of their foes perished in one of the worst scourges ever visited on the esteemed Chinese bureaucracy.

After inaugurating the Song dynasty, Zhao moved to curb the power of eunuchs by limiting them to the role of servants. Later rulers and regents of the dynasty would periodically restore eunuchs to positions of trust and influence, but overall they counted for less under the Song than the palace women— including not only the emperor's principal and secondary wives but also his vast corps of female retainers. The number of such women employed by the emperor increased from more than 200 in Zhao's day to more than 2,000 later in the dynasty, all of whom

## DISTINCTIVE ATTIRE

In fashion as in other things, the Chinese valued simplicity and restraint, and people of all ranks dressed rather conservatively. Nonetheless, men and women of distinction proclaimed their status by wearing clothes that tastefully set them apart from those of lesser importance. But fashion rules were flexible enough to allow for some exotic flourishes, particularly among women who entertained the emperor and other prominent men.

Top officials signaled their rank by the color of the robe they wore—with purple being the most prestigious shade, followed by crimson. In addition, high-ranking men sometimes attached lifts to their shoes so that they would appear taller and took great pride in the straight "feet" on their caps, whereas lower-ranking men wore caps with curved or crossed feet.

Fashionable women were distinguished by their delicate

Quiet elegance was the height of fashion, as seen in this gathering of distinguished men in handsome gowns, entertained by a neatly coiffured lute player and by serving women in soft-colored robes.

Men of various ranks wore caps like this one, with feet stiffened with wire or bamboo so they could be displayed straight, curved, or crossed, according to one's status.

robes, blouses, and capes made of expensive fabrics, such as silk, and by their fancy coiffures, including buns more than a foot tall and adorned with pins and combs shaped like flowers, birds, phoenixes, or butterflies. Not every woman who dressed in such high style was necessarily of aristocratic birth. Women of plain background but uncommon allure were sometimes recruited as singers, dancers, or serving women to appear at the palace in exquisite attire before the emperor and his guests. Such women helped set the standard for beauty with their slender figures, pale skin (enhanced by cosmetics), and dainty feet. One notorious fashion trend—the practice of foot-binding—began among dancing women at court before becoming the vogue among the aristocracy and spreading to the population at large.

A maid wearing a plain gown *(far left)* helps two fashionable women in finer apparel and fancier hairdos complete their makeup.

This beauty kit includes pots for powders and other cosmetics; combs and brushes; and tweezers *(far right)*, used to remove the eyebrows, which were then redrawn.

## FOOT-BINDING

Foot-binding was first practiced on girls training to be palace dancers, to make their feet daintier and more appealing. Such light-footed dancers and actresses, like the pair in pointed slippers at left, charmed the emperor and other men of high rank and started an unfortunate trend. During the Song dynasty, aristocrats began binding the feet of their young daughters simply to make the girls more desirable and marriageable.

Over time, the ideal foot size became smaller and the binding more crippling. The slippers below were fashioned in the 13th century for bound feet scarcely five inches long. Ultimately, the goal became a foot length of about three inches, resulting in a broken instep and toes that were permanently curled under. Women deformed in this way could not even walk properly, and bound feet became a symbol of female submission.

lived and worked on the palace grounds. Overseeing them was an imposing matron known as the Supreme Commander of the Palace, who administered six bureaus of female retainers, including one devoted to rites and etiquette, another to clothing, and a third to food and wine.

The women in these bureaus were largely concerned with serving the emperor and his retinue, but their duties were not strictly menial. The palace actively recruited women who could read and write and conducted remedial classes for retainers who lacked education. Not every woman at court needed to be literate, but the emperor and other men of the ruling class liked to have cultivated women around them. Other talents that might earn a woman distinction at court included skill as a musician, a flair for cooking or fashioning garments, or a gift for healing (palace women who fell ill were usually treated by a female specialist from the Department of Medicine, a subdivision of the Bureau of Food and Wine).

Women serving at court had more than one avenue of advancement. They could climb the ladder within their bureau to a higher grade, for they were ranked in the same manner as male civil servants. A woman who rose to become head of her bureau, for example, acquired a rank equal to that of a man who served in the provinces as a regional supervisor. In some cases, a female retainer might catch the eye of the emperor and be asked to join his harem, whose members were themselves ranked on an ascending scale, ranging from relatively lowly designations such as Talented One to the lofty title of Noble Consort. A few women of common origins who entered the palace as mere retainers soared all the way to the top to become empresses.

A woman who hoped to attract the emperor's attention might do well to land a job in the Bureau of Rites and Etiquette, whose staff of 50 or so retainers provided music for

A kneeling man prepares to kowtow to a superior by touching his head to the ground in this 12th-century painting. Paying respect to authority figures as well as to one's parents and ancestors was extolled by Confucius as "the basis of virtue and the source of all instruction."

imperial ceremonies and saw to it that every ritual unfolded properly, from the opening procession to the final bow. These were crucial details, for the ceremonies that the emperor took part in were considered as important to the welfare of China as the decrees he issued or the policies he sanctioned. In rituals, the Son of Heaven served as an intermediary between the people on earth and the spirits on high, seeking blessings for China and replenishing the realm. Such were his duties on New Year's Day, which coincided with the second new moon after the winter solstice. At dawn, the emperor burned incense in a temple at the palace and prayed for bountiful harvests in the year to come before receiving greetings and gifts from a host of emissaries.

New Year's Day was just the beginning of a joyous period that culminated some two weeks later with the boisterous Feast of Lanterns, when people bedecked their homes, shops, and squares with lamps and stayed up all night, drinking and singing. The highlight of the revelry at Kaifeng was a great show presided over by the emperor and staged atop a large wooden platform. Across that stage danced glowing dragons propelled by men with lanterns, which cast a ghostly light through the thin green cloth sheathing the fabricated monsters.

More admired than feared, dragons symbolized the emperor and his awesome power. In this season of hope and anticipation, people trusted that their ruler would use that power wisely and bring them good fortune—and that for all his privileges, he would continue to deal with them generously, fulfilling the promise inscribed on a banner near the stage: "The emperor shares his pleasures with the people."

The Chinese New Year was an occasion for families to gather in celebration, and men whose duties kept them apart from their parents at other times made every effort to join them for the festivities. One worthy administrator by the name of Wang, who entered the civil service in 1015, was so devoted to his parents that he took them with him to every post he was assigned to—with the exception of one district so remote that he was obliged to leave his mother and father behind. Bereft of their company, Wang declined to take part in any banquets or celebrations. When the New Year arrived and others exulted, he shunned the revelry and pined for his distant parents.

Such wholehearted adherence to the Confucian ideal of filial piety made a deep impression on the official's son Wang Anshi, who entered the civil service himself as a young man and rose to become one of the most important and controversial figures of his age. After his father died in 1039, Wang Anshi com-posed a memorial to him, praising his virtues as a family man and an administrator. Once when a senior official complained of late tax payments by people in the district he was overseeing, the elder Wang replied that it was "useless to blame the lower classes as long as the government employees continued to set them a bad example." Aided by an army officer, he arrested all the government clerks who had fallen behind in their taxes, gave them each 20 strokes with a bamboo rod, and allowed them just three days to pay up. Thereafter, people in the district gave the tax collectors no cause for complaint.

Much like his father, Wang Anshi warmly embraced tradition in some respects but challenged the way things were done in other regards. He cherished the old Confucian ideal of a society where children and parents, disciples and masters, subjects and rulers were linked by reciprocal bonds of filial respect and paternal devotion. But to achieve such elusive social harmony and strengthen the state, he proposed major changes in the way that China was governed. Some of those measures proved as jarring to his colleagues and critics as his father's blunt method of tax reform did to the clerks. Before his career was through, Wang was denounced by many of his peers—the gifted corps of administrators who were not simply officials but scholars, guardians of the proud Chinese tradition that based leadership on learning.

Wang Anshi himself was among the brightest of the scholars. Born in 1021, he was the third of 10 children—seven brothers and three sisters—a heavy responsibility for his father, who lacked the inherited wealth of others in his position (many scholar-officials were prosperous landowners). Nonetheless, young Wang and two of his brothers achieved prominence and must have been given a first-rate education, a lengthy process that usually began at home and continued at a government-run school or a private academy, sometimes culminating under the tutelage of a leading scholar at the National University in Kaifeng.

Pupils first had to master the Chinese language and its myr-

## THE EVOLUTION OF WRITING

Although lovely to behold, Chinese writing was difficult to learn, and even the most diligent young scholars could spend many years attempting to master its intricacies. The difficulty lay in the vast number of characters—at least 10,000 in Song times—and in the many complex ways that those characters could be combined to convey ideas.

Unlike the concise phonetic alphabet that the Romans bequeathed to western Europe, in which each character represents a sound in the spoken language, many Chinese characters represent an object or a concept, but it is depicted in an abstract form. As illustrated at right, the character representing *fish* originated in ancient times as a schematic picture of a fish *(top)*. But over the centuries, as writers switched from a hard-pointed stylus to a soft-haired brush, that character became more flowing and abstract until it arrived at the form in use during the Song period *(bottom)*, which required only a few quick strokes with the brush but bore no resemblance to a fish.

Once the aspiring scholar-officials mastered the cryptic characters as well as their sundry combinations, however, they had a powerful tool at their disposal. Although Chinese dialects varied greatly from one region to another, the written language was universal, enabling an administrator from the far south, for example, to communicate readily with one from the far north. For the rulers of a sprawling empire that sometimes threatened to come apart at the seams, the written language served as a great unifier, one that held the officials together, if not the people they governed.

iad characters. Then they were steeped in the classics, including the teachings of Confucius and his leading interpreters, the historical commentaries of the preeminent scholar-officials of past dynasties, and the lyrics of the great poets. Students memorized, copied, and reflected on those classics, using books that were being produced in ever greater numbers across China thanks to recent advances in printing.

Once pupils were versed in the classics, they were ready to compose their own prose and lyrics, laden with allusions to the masterpieces they had learned by heart and penned in a calligraphy that constituted an art form in itself. Wang Anshi was soon recognized as an exceptional student, with a prodigious memory and a quick hand. "In composing he wrote so fast that the pen seemed to fly over the paper," wrote one scholar in tribute to him, "and although he seemed to be exercising no particular care, the work when completed was remarkable for content and style."

What came so easily to Wang left other students baffled or stultified. Some rebelled against the grind with a flourish. One 10-year-old boy ran away from the boarding school his parents sent him to and ended up in a local school, which he found just as intolerable. When he stubbornly refused to learn to read or write, his teacher whipped him. That night, in a rage, the youngster set the school ablaze with his teacher inside (the man barely escaped in time). Any hopes the boy had for a career as an official went up in smoke, but he found his calling in the military, eventually rising to the rank of general.

By the age of 20, Wang Anshi was ready to face the supreme test of a scholar—the grueling civil service examination that would make or break him. To replenish the bureaucracy with talented young men from throughout China, Song rulers had expanded that examination system. Local exams were now administered in each of China's 300 or so districts, and those who scored highest were sent to Kaifeng for further testing. The proportion of China's officials who earned their places through the examination system had risen from about 15 percent to roughly 30 percent. Others acquired jobs through a practice known as "protection," which permitted high-ranking officials to name one or more of their relatives to government posts. But many young men eligible for protection preferred to vie for distinction in the exams.

Precocious scholars like Wang Anshi usually faced that test in early adulthood, but there were no age limits, and those who failed were free to try again. The average age of exam takers was 35, and some kept at it doggedly well into their sixties. Tens of thousands came forward each time the exams were held—every three years or so—but in any one sitting only

Calligraphers in Song times used plainer versions of the writing tools shown here, produced later, during the Ming period. The brush, of wolf hair with a lacquered wooden handle inlaid with mother-of-pearl, was dipped in the shallow recess of the ink stone, which was filled with ink made of soot mixed with a small amount of water.

about 250 passed the highest tier of tests in the capital, a feat that guaranteed them illustrious and lucrative careers. Once in a while, so few men passed that the losers ran riot, even dousing an effigy of the chief examiner with blood on one occasion. Women were excluded from the exams, as were men who had worked as artisans, merchants, or clerks—activities considered unfit for scholars—and Buddhist or Daoist monks. (In fact, many Confucian scholars were influenced by Buddhism and Daoism, but men exclusively devoted to either faith were discouraged from running government affairs.)

While preparing for the examination at Kaifeng, Wang Anshi befriended another candidate who had taken the test there once before and failed. Despite that setback, he impressed Wang as a true scholar, one who had the gift to enlighten others. "I was spurred on to imitation of him," Wang later wrote. "We began to exchange poems, through each of which breathed a spirit of frank and happy comradeship. Through my friendship with him I first became conscious of the possibility of becoming a worthy disciple of the ancient sages."

Such comradeship helped prepare him for the exams, which tested not only the candidate's knowledge but also his moral and poetic qualities. He might be asked to compose verse that evoked "the sound of the oars, and the green of the hills and water." Or he might have to expound in prose on this definition of leadership from a disciple of Confucius: "To possess ability, and yet ask of those who do not; to know much, and yet inquire of those who know little; to possess, and yet appear not to possess; to be full, and yet appear empty." A man who could heed those words might indeed make a good official in a land where few people could even dream of such privileges as the scholars enjoyed.

Sadly, Wang's friend failed the examination at Kaifeng a second time and drowned on his way home from the capital. By contrast, Wang not only passed on his first attempt but placed fourth among that year's successful candidates. At the age of 21, he received the coveted degree of *jinshi,* or "advanced scholar."

His critics later charged improbably that he owed his success in the exams to the influence of friends at court, an abuse that sometimes occurred, despite efforts to discourage favoritism and cheating. Each candidate at Kaifeng took the big three-day exam in a separate cubicle, where he remained throughout the ordeal. He provided his own food and bedding, which proctors searched as a precaution against cribbing. Exam papers were identified by number rather than by name, and clerks recopied all the papers to prevent examiners from identifying the authors by their hand-

Successful young scholars like Wang were eagerly sought after as husbands. Some parents of eligible girls would study the published list of successful candidates and compete for the top finishers by offering them large dowries. Although love matches were not unheard of in China, marriage among members of the ruling class was largely a practical matter—an alliance in which the interests of the two families took precedence over the feelings of the bride and groom. Marriage talks were often initiated by matchmakers: women skilled in the art of assessing the merits and requirements of the two sides and arranging terms. In some cases, the bride might not even meet the groom until the day of the wedding, when she rode to her husband's home in a litter with her face veiled and became part of his family, bound by the same obligation of piety to his parents as he was.

Every father wanted sons if only because they enhanced the family by bringing wives

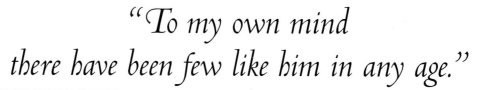

## "To my own mind there have been few like him in any age."

writing and favoring those they knew. Two examiners graded each paper independently, and a third examiner would then reconcile any difference between the two marks. Only those who passed that anonymous test were invited to the palace for a final, less arduous exam, held in front of the emperor and used primarily to rank the successful candidates—some of whom might be known to those at court and perhaps favored as a result.

But it appears Wang Anshi achieved a high ranking through his own merits and did little to ingratiate himself with those in power. As one admirer said, "He has already gained his jinshi degree, but is known to very few people. As a matter of fact, he is not anxious to get known. He is a sincere and self-respecting person. To my own mind there have been few like him in any age."

and children into the home. But daughters were cherished as well. When Wang Anshi was a young married man in his mid-twenties, his infant daughter died, and he grieved deeply, composing a tribute to her that praised her intelligence and promise. Leading families often fulfilled such promise by instructing their daughters so that they might marry gifted scholars who prized learning in their wives.

Wang had surviving children to care for and public responsibilities to fulfill. After serving an apprenticeship as an under secretary, he was promoted to magistrate—a district governor whose duties included not only resolving disputes as a judge but also maintaining order, overseeing tax collection, and supervising public works. Scrupulous magistrates like Wang did all they could

Scholars complete the final stage of the civil service examination, held at the palace
under the eye of the emperor *(seated at center table)*. Those who reached this stage had
already passed two demanding tests and were virtually assured of earning their
degrees and becoming prominent officials.

to improve the lot of those under them, realizing that a government that simply took from the people and offered them nothing in return would soon lose its moral authority.

Wang's district was situated in southern China, near the sea, and had long been plagued by alternating droughts and floods because the streams and channels that carried water to the fields had been neglected. Unless cleared of silt regularly, such waterways became clogged in dry seasons and overflowed in wet seasons. Fortunately, the weather was good and the harvests bountiful when Wang arrived in the district, and he encouraged farmers to take advantage of the respite and improve the drainage system. Under his leadership, they cleared and deepened the channels, raised dikes, drained marshes, and built reservoirs to hold floodwaters for use in times of drought. Such efforts eased the hardships of farmers, but they were still subject to poor harvests periodically. In times of want, Wang loaned grain to those in need, to be repaid in kind with interest after the next harvest, thus replenishing the government granaries that served as reserves against famine.

Attended by servants and family members, scholar-officials compose poetry together on a spring day, with each guest adding a verse to match the efforts of the others. So privileged that they never had to use their hands for anything other than painting or writing, some scholars let the nails on their little fingers grow very long in order to show how little acquainted they were with manual labor.

These measures were both popular and successful, earning Wang the lasting gratitude of the people in his district, who would long honor his memory at shrines. His good work also won him favor in Kaifeng. After his four-year term as magistrate was over, however, Wang astonished his friends by returning home rather than reporting to Kaifeng, as requested by the reigning emperor, Renzong, to take a special examination for a high government post in the capital. Such a position carried with it a one-year unpaid probationary period, and Wang felt a financial responsibility to his wife and children as well as to his mother and other family members who had relied on him for support since his father died. Wang implored the emperor in writing to allow him to place their interests first and serve another term as a salaried official in the provinces.

A lesser talent might have spoiled his prospects by refusing a call from the emperor, but Wang was allowed to remain in the provinces and even granted a promotion. He subsequently fended off another summons to the capital, leading some to suspect that he was trying to pique the interest of his superiors at court by playing hard to get. Whatever his reasons for shunning Kaifeng, he used his time in the provinces well, testing out reforms that he would later implement throughout China—measures aimed at protecting farmers from inefficient and sometimes corrupt administrators and from avaricious merchants who made loans to farmers at exorbitantly high interest rates.

Finally, in 1060, Emperor Renzong waived the requirements for both the examination and the unpaid probationary period and ordered Wang, now almost 40 years old, to the capital. During the next three years, he served with some reluctance in a series of ever more prestigious positions, including Imperial Librarian, Keeper of the Emperor's Diary, and Supervisor of Justice. He had joined the emperor's inner circle, but he remained fiercely independent, often challenging more-seasoned officials.

As Supervisor of Justice, for example, he overruled a veteran lower court judge who had sentenced a young man to death for killing a friend during a scuffle over a fighting quail. The victim had stolen the quail from the accused man, and Wang ruled that he should not be condemned for a justifiable attempt to retrieve that property. The lower court judge, incensed that Wang, a palace newcomer, had dared to contradict him, appealed the case to the Chief Court of Justice, which ruled in favor of the lower court judge and demanded from Wang a public apology. He flatly refused to apologize—and the emperor did not press him to do so, thus signaling that Wang retained support in the court that mattered most.

Emperor Renzong died a short time later, in 1063, after almost 40 years on the throne. He was succeeded by his nephew, Yingzong, whom Wang served for only a few months before leaving office and returning home to mourn the death of his mother. Confucian teachings prescribed a three-year period of mourning for the death of a parent, and Wang insisted on fulfilling that obligation, despite repeated appeals from court for him to return to Kaifeng. (An official might cut his mourning short under such circumstances, but if he concealed the news of a parent's death to avoid leaving office for a decent period of mourning, he was subject to scorn.) Even after his mourning ended, Wang refused to return to the capital, requesting an assignment near his home instead. He cited family concerns and ill health, but he may also have felt that the reforms he favored had little chance of being embraced by the new emperor.

Only after Yingzong died in 1067 and his 20-year-old son, Shenzong, took the throne did Wang consent to return to Kai-

## HONORING THE ANCESTORS

In imperial China, the death of a relative elevated the deceased to the status of an honored ancestor, to whom the living owed funeral offerings and a lengthy period of mourning, lasting up to three years in the case of a parent. Such rituals reflected the ancient belief that the spirits of the ancestors lingered after death and had to be appeased with reverent gestures, including prayers and offerings made at altars in the home and at the gravesite.

To house their deceased kin, wealthy families built grand tombs, complete with hallways and rooms. The tombs were stocked with gifts of wine or rice in decorative urns (below) and adorned with scenes of ease and contentment like the relief at right, which shows a husband and wife seated placidly at a table. In addition, mourners honored and protected ancestral spirits by placing servant figures at their grave sites and lining the approach to the tomb with stone or ceramic beasts to guard the "spirit way."

feng. Young Shenzong had high hopes. Earlier Song rulers had succeeded in rebuilding a formidable empire, but China remained threatened by powerful foes, notably the Khitans to the north, who were adept at mounted warfare. Shenzong wanted to strengthen his state against such rivals and expand its borders. Yet how was he to achieve this without placing an intolerable burden on the peasantry, already overtaxed and subject to conscription for long terms as laborers and soldiers?

Shenzong was no tyrant. As an official chronicler noted, he tried to live up to the Confucian ideal of the benevolent ruler, "merciful to the poor and aged, and generous to the distressed." He recognized in Wang Anshi someone who shared his ambition to strengthen China without devastating the already afflicted peasantry—who believed, in fact, that the same measures that helped the poor would also serve the larger interests of the empire. In 1069, over the bitter opposition of some of his most powerful advisers, Shenzong appointed Wang to his Grand Council, and Wang soon emerged as the emperor's chief councilor.

Wang Anshi was not yet 50 and had spent little of his career in the capital. But it was not his inexperience that bothered his critics as much as his unconventional ways. Unlike most officials, who prided themselves on their appearance, Wang was careless about his dress and other points of etiquette. It was said that he seldom bathed, never changed his gown, and ate anything that was placed before him, hardly noticing what it was. His friends forgave such oddities, reasoning that he was preoccupied with great thoughts. But his foes regarded such bad form as a sign of bad character. "It is natural for a man to want to wash his face when it is dirty and to send his filthy garments to the laundry," wrote one of his detractors. "Not so with this man! He wears a barbarian's robe and eats the food of pigs and dogs and discusses poetry and history with a convict's unshaved head and unwashed face. Now is this natural? A man who does not act according to human nature must be a great hypocrite and a scheming intriguer."

Wang Anshi made no concessions to his critics. Another man might have tried to appease his opponents before embarking on ambitious reforms. But Wang had always been sure of his own judgment and unfazed by the objections of others, and he forged ahead with a program that shook the venerable framework of the Chinese state to its foundations.

As chief councilor, Wang Anshi promptly introduced a series of measures known as the New Policies, rooted in the principle that the government should take more responsibility for the welfare of its citizens—in particular, the poor people of the countryside, who were at risk of "being ground into the dust by the rich," Wang declared. He hoped to ease the debts that those at the bottom of society owed to those above them, so that the poor would render better service to China and bolster the state.

Among the ways in which he worked to achieve that goal was to reform the punishing system by which the government conscripted laborers for such vital tasks as building roads and dredging waterways. Initially, men had been required to serve without pay on public projects for no more than three days a year. But by Wang's time, conscripts often toiled for much longer periods, during which they were unable to support their families and had to meet their own expenses—a prospect so ruinous that some men committed suicide rather than comply. Merchants or clerks might have to perform lighter tasks for the government, but most of the hard labor was done by farmers, who could ill afford to be absent long from their fields. Although they were supposed to labor for the benefit of all, they sometimes toiled for a precious few. In one case, 200 farmers were sent to Kaifeng to serve as stableboys at the palace.

Wang Anshi replaced this system with one that taxed families according to their

During the Song period, scholar-officials avidly collected and studied Chinese antiquities made thousands of years earlier, like this bronze wine vessel, portrayed in a woodcut with accompanying text from a printed catalog describing the collection.

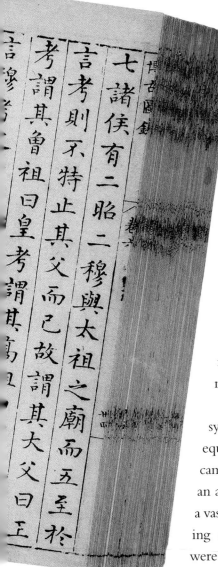

wealth and used the proceeds to hire men for public works. His program met with resistance from the wealthy, who were always looking for ways to avoid taxation and counted on help in that regard from compliant officials. Nonetheless, Wang succeeded in raising enough money and hiring enough laborers to carry on with the most pressing of tasks—the dredging of China's major waterways to guard against flooding and ease navigation. Even some critics who faulted Wang's other reforms conceded that the new labor system was an improvement over the old regime.

Wang's efforts to reform China's system of national defense were equally ambitious. At the time he became chief councilor, China possessed an army of more than a million men—a vast force, to be sure, but one with glaring deficiencies. Many of the soldiers were lackluster conscripts from the countryside, more adept at farming than at fighting, and few were equipped to compete on horseback with China's mounted foes to the north. Wang set out to create a smaller but more efficient army—one that would be less of a drain on the treasury—and to supplement that regular force with a vast militia.

Throughout China, he established local militia units to which every family with more than one male of fighting age had to provide one soldier. On average, each soldier served for about a month each year, but the units as a whole remained active for much of the year, functioning as local police forces and as reserves for the army in wartime. The families of the militiamen were themselves organized into groups, each with a headman who served as chief of police and investigated crimes. This system helped to reduce banditry and other offenses, but the militia was never tested in war and its effectiveness remained a matter of speculation. As promised, Wang pared down the regular army to roughly half its former size but bolstered the cavalry by requiring families in northern provinces, where the grazing was good and the danger from foreign invaders acute, to tend government-supplied horses for the army.

These reforms demanded more of the populace than Wang's changes in the labor system did. Fewer farmers now had to forsake their fields to serve in the regular army, but many more had to interrupt their chores to perform stints in the militia, which grew to a size of more than seven million men during Wang's tenure. Complaints arose about the inconvenience of the system and about misconduct by those in charge of the militia.

Wang stirred up even stronger objections with his sweeping economic reforms. Like any shrewd administrator, he began by scrutinizing the government's annual budget, examining every expenditure for waste. He sliced state expenses by 40 percent and demanded that all monies be accounted for, thus reducing the graft that fattened the purses of corrupt officials. But he was not content with such economies. He believed that too much of China's wealth was going to greedy merchants and lenders, and he proposed that the government assume many of their functions for its own benefit and for the good of the poor.

Chinese farmers had long relied on loans from local merchants to make ends meet, particularly at planting time in the spring, when their resources were low and their needs were great.

So desperate were the farmers for help that they agreed to pay lenders annual interest rates of up to 50 percent, at the risk of losing their farms if they defaulted. Expanding on a program he had instituted as a local official, Wang set up a national rural aid program called Green Sprouts, in which the government served as lender to needy farmers in the spring. The farmers repaid those loans with interest after the fall harvest. Destitute peasants received free land as well as loans and were expected to repay the government with interest once the land generated a profit.

Green Sprouts failed to yield the bounty Wang hoped for. To meet the expenses of the program, he set the annual interest rate on the loans at 24 percent—less than private lenders had charged but still too steep for many farmers to meet when harvests fell

To some extent, Sima's conservatism reflected his privileged status. He came from a more prosperous and prestigious family than Wang, and his father, a high-ranking figure at court, had invoked "protection" to bring him into the civil service, although he later passed the examination in Kaifeng and earned his degree. Unlike Wang, he did not serve long in the provinces but chose instead a post in Kaifeng. Like others of his class, he believed that established, wealthy families were best positioned to run things in the capital as well as in the countryside.

Yet there was more to his philosophy than self-interest. Like Wang, Sima subscribed to the Confucian doctrine that the people would prosper only if their rulers were virtuous and benevolent. In his view, however, the essence of virtuous leadership was not

# "Those who oppose him are despised as vilifiers and slanderers."

short of expectations. Local officials were supposed to forgive all or part of the loans in lean years, but some failed to do so. Instead they pressured farmers to renew their loans and fall deeper into debt or took advantage of their plight in other ways.

Wang's opponents seized on these problems as symptomatic of his various reforms, which they saw as fundamentally misguided. For Sima Guang, a conservative councilor and historian who emerged as Wang's leading critic, the real shame was not that some local officials administering his programs were callous but that the state had no business involving itself so deeply in the affairs of the people. Matters of profit and loss were better left to merchants, he believed, than to officials who would only demean themselves and disillusion the populace by playing a role for which they were unsuited.

to change the social order but to preserve it. In studying China's history, he found cautionary examples of rulers and councilors whose overambitious plans of conquest or reform brought grave disturbances to China. The traditional order of society might not satisfy such reckless dreamers, Sima concluded, but it was infinitely preferable to chaos. He feared that Wang was one of those rash reformers who in striving to "make everything new" risked severing the age-old ties that linked the rich to the poor and rulers to their subjects. The failure of Green Sprouts, he believed, was the sort of misfortune that inevitably resulted when rulers ignored time-honored precedents and lost their way.

Wang, for his part, attributed the problems he encountered to errors on the part of local officials rather than to flaws in his own design and believed that much worse would befall China if

Bull-drawn carts laden with goods wind their way up a mountain path in this 12th-century scroll painting. Commerce flourished during the Song dynasty as the population increased and the demand for goods surged. In addition, merchants transporting their wares benefited greatly from such public works projects as the building of roads and the dredging of rivers and canals.

the leadership failed to address the great problems facing the state. Although his dispute with Sima Guang was sharp, the two men continued to correspond with each other and recognized that theirs was a conflict of principle. In one letter, Sima blasted Wang's policies but conceded that both sides were motivated by a genuine desire to help the people: "Although our directions are different, we have the same goal."

Sima and his fellow conservatives constantly complained to Emperor Shenzong about Wang and his reforms. Sometimes they voiced their concerns directly to Shenzong at court, and at other times they addressed him in memorials, or long written documents. When Shenzong remained steadfast in his support of Wang, many of the critics either resigned or asked to be transferred to positions in the provinces. Sima himself made such a request in 1071. "You now rely solely upon the counsel of Wang Anshi," he wrote the emperor. "Those who are of one mind with him are regarded as good and loyal servants of the throne, but those who oppose him are despised as vilifiers and slanderers." He added that if the emperor regarded him as in any way blameworthy, "then shall I meekly await your sentence of banishment or death." Neither fate befell him. He was transferred to a distant post, where he patiently awaited a shift in the political winds.

Although Wang Anshi had no desire to make martyrs of his opponents, he was glad to see them dismissed or dispatched to remote provinces. Indeed, one of the traits that most disturbed his foes was his intolerance of dissent. He was denounced for seeking the resignation or reassignment of nettlesome imperial censors, who were supposed to be free with their criticism. And in reforming the educational system, he tried to impose his own interpretations of the classics, leading to charges that he was stifling independent thinking among would-be scholar-officials.

Wang may have been overzealous in promoting his policies, but not to the point that he silenced the opposition. Memorials attacking him continued to reach the emperor, and eventually the

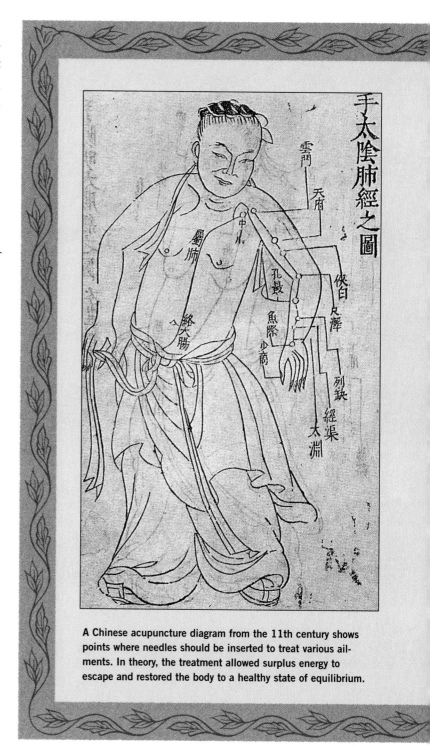

A Chinese acupuncture diagram from the 11th century shows points where needles should be inserted to treat various ailments. In theory, the treatment allowed surplus energy to escape and restored the body to a healthy state of equilibrium.

# RESTORING HEALTH AND HARMONY

Like the scholar-officials who treated China's social ills, healers in the Song period believed that curing ailments was essentially a philosophical problem. They saw the body as a world with its own rules and rhythms. When those rhythms were disturbed, illness resulted. Doctors argued over whether the causes were internal or external, but all agreed that the goal of treatment was to restore bodily harmony.

The ancient Chinese practice of acupuncture, for example, was an attempt to regain equilibrium between *yin* (the passive, or female, force) and *yang* (the active, or male, force) by penetrating with needles the many points associated with one force or the other and releasing excess energy until balance was achieved. In pursuing this theoretical goal, acupuncturists gained practical knowledge of anatomy and the nervous system—refining their skills on wax-coated models of the human figure filled with mercury—and succeeded in treating various pains and disorders.

Moxibustion *(below),* the application of heat to an afflicted area, originated in similar fashion, as an effort to correct an imbalance within the body. Although the practice yielded fewer medical benefits than acupuncture, it did serve to cauterize areas and prevent infection. Other healers of the day, meanwhile, were contributing new herbal remedies to China's already impressive pharmacopoeia, providing patients with fresh options in their quest for health and harmony.

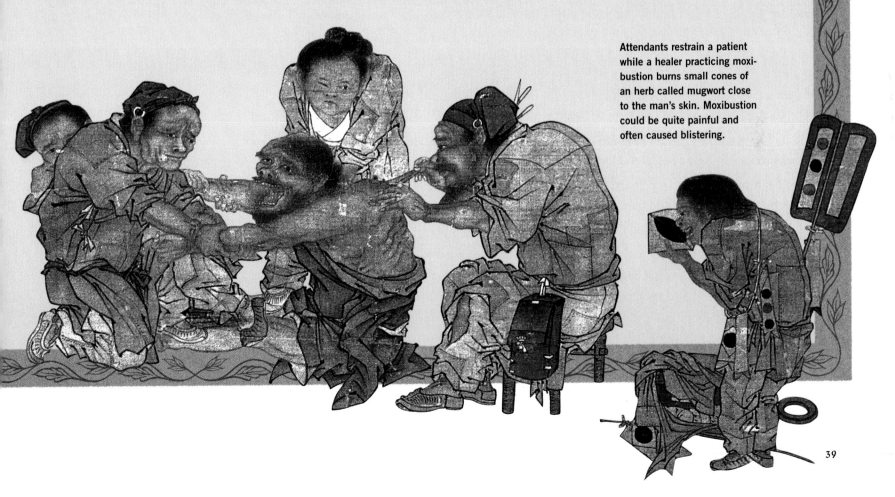

Attendants restrain a patient while a healer practicing moxibustion burns small cones of an herb called mugwort close to the man's skin. Moxibustion could be quite painful and often caused blistering.

critics succeeded in shaking Shenzong's confidence in him. Their arguments were reinforced by a series of natural disasters—first an earthquake, then a plague of locusts, and finally a long and ruinous drought. Wang's opponents interpreted those calamities as signs that the Son of Heaven had followed the wrong path and upset the natural order. Finally, in 1074, as the drought entered its seventh month, the emperor grew anxious and informed Wang that to placate the heavens and bring rain, he was considering repealing all measures that might be unjust and were causing unrest, including some of the New Policies.

Wang appealed to the emperor's reason. "Floods and droughts occur in the ordinary course of nature," he argued. "All that is necessary is that the government should do all in its power to relieve the people." But Shenzong felt obliged to atone for the misfortunes afflicting his people—a feeling heightened by a memorial he received from a provincial official who described in grim detail the plight of starving refugees fleeing from China's drought-stricken northeast. Once a friend of Wang's, the official now fixed the blame for China's plight squarely on the chief councilor's shoulders. "The drought is caused by Wang Anshi," he assured the emperor. "If you dismiss him, and if rain does not fall within ten days afterwards, you may cut off my head."

The emperor sighed when he read that memorial, placed it up the sleeve of his robe, and retired to his bedchamber, where he found no rest. The following morning, he ordered the temporary suspension of several of the New Policies. Within hours, it was said, a heavy rain fell, breaking the drought. Critics of the reforms flocked to the emperor's side to congratulate him on his wise action. A short time later, Wang Anshi resigned.

Although Wang was no doubt dismayed by the emperor's decision, he was also in ill health and longed to return home, having spent six stressful years implementing reforms in the face of fierce opposition. He often felt dizzy and was short of breath. Shenzong remained loyal to Wang and his reforms, restoring the

New Policies in full after the crisis had passed. But Wang no longer had the strength to lead the fight. After returning to Kaifeng for a while at the emperor's urging, he left the capital for good.

Wang ultimately settled down at a small house in the country, where he planted 300 trees and dug a fish pond. He later donated the property to a Buddhist temple, asking the priests there to pray daily for the souls of his parents and a beloved son who had died a few years earlier. He spent the rest of his days reading and writing, far from the public limelight—a retirement of the sort many officials looked forward to and regarded as the fulfillment of the scholarly life. Wang's retirement may have been tinged with some bitterness, but the emperor stayed in touch with his old friend, bestowing upon him many honors and a generous pension. He also made sure that Wang received the best medical care, sending court physicians to his bedside when his health began to fail. Shenzong himself fell sick and died in 1085, and Wang Anshi passed away the next year, leaving a legacy of reform that would be debated ever after by those who watched over China.

By the time Shenzong died, the heated controversy over Wang Anshi and his New Policies had engulfed the imperial household. The palace eunuchs had long resented Wang because he urged the emperor to bar them from positions of influence. They and other opponents of reform found a champion in Shenzong's mother, who had warned her son on one occasion that a comet that appeared in the night sky was an omen of the disaster awaiting China if he continued to follow Wang's evil ways. After Shenzong's death, it was she who served as regent to his young son and heir, Zhezong, and who ran the country as dowager empress. She lost no time in ridding the court of Wang's supporters and replacing them with his foes,

notably Sima Guang, who, despite old age and ill health, eagerly returned to Kaifeng and dismantled the New Policies. Wang lived just long enough to see his proudest achievement, paid labor for public works, scrapped, along with his other initiatives.

Sima survived Wang by only five months, but the power struggle between reformers and conservatives did not end with the deaths of those two great antagonists. Young Zhezong shared his late father's views and longed for the day when he would emerge from under the shadow of his conservative grandmother. He and his backers thought that time had come when he turned 17. But the empress dowager clung to power for another year before death brought an end to her regency. No sooner had Zhezong assumed the throne than he reinstituted reforms, but officials in the provinces resisted those changes. In the end, little was done to address China's festering problems, including an army that remained ill prepared to deal with China's powerful enemies to the north and an imperial treasury that demanded too little from the rich and too much from the beleaguered peasants.

Zhezong's reign was cut short by his death in 1100, and he was succeeded by his 17-year-old half brother, Huizong, whose luxurious tastes and artistic temperament left him unsuited for the hard challenges that lay ahead. Like his predecessors, he favored reform, but he only hurt that cause by persecuting conservatives and alienating many within the bureaucracy. Frustrated by politics, he sought refuge in more aesthetic pursuits. He excelled at calligraphy, poetry, and painting, known as the three perfections; artists often combined these skills to produce haunting scenes graced with beautifully inscribed lines of verse. His delicate paintings of flowers and birds were among the finest produced during the Song dynasty. He founded China's first academy of painting, added drawing tests to the jinshi exam, and published a 20-volume catalog of the paintings in the Imperial Gallery—most of which were later destroyed when the enemy forces he failed to deter sacked Kaifeng.

Huizong's most extravagant work was a huge royal pleasure park he created in Kaifeng on the advice of a Daoist priest renowned for his ability to cure illnesses with talismans and to exorcise demons. The priest promised him that undertaking such a noble project would ensure him many sons, and soon after embarking on the task, Huizong fathered the first of more than two dozen sons by one or another of his 19 consorts.

His pleasure park contained precious rocks, rare plants, and a host of exotic animals gathered from the far corners of the empire. Its centerpiece was a man-made mountain more than 90 feet tall with twin peaks. Water cascaded down the mountain slope into a serene pool haunted by flocks of geese and ducks. Among the other creatures roaming the park were gibbons—who roused Kaifeng's residents in the night with their howling—thousands of deer, and a mysterious beast reported to have no head, eyes, or feet and a thunderous roar.

The emperor spared no expense to stock the park with wondrous specimens. "Common people were dispatched to search around cliffs and sift through swamps," noted one contemporary. "Mountains were hacked to pieces and rocks were carted away." As many as 30 ships were commandeered to transport treasures to the park. A huge cargo ship was built from scratch to carry one immense boulder thought to have divine significance from a distant lake to Kaifeng. As the ship moved north toward the capital along rivers and canals, workers tore down bridges and other barriers barring its progress. Others assigned to stock the imperial pleasure park did more than destroy public property; they pillaged homes and businesses and forced villagers to collect specimens, punishing them mercilessly if they failed to deliver as ordered.

This was a far cry from the benevolence that sages had long urged upon emperors as the key to preserving social harmony. But Huizong was a poor judge of character, and he relied heavily on the advice of two cronies—his chief councilor and an ambitious court eunuch—who were too busy enhancing their own positions to instruct him in the moral obligations of leadership. To make matters worse, construction of the pleasure park and other extravagant projects forced Huizong to hike taxes, which fell heavily on the

Twenty cranes, symbolizing good fortune and longevity, circle over the palace in this painting attributed to Huizong, the last Song emperor to rule China from Kaifeng before northern invaders descended on the city. Like many emperors, Huizong put great stock in the power of omens and interpreted this sight, which he witnessed, as a blessing from heaven upon his reign.

him from tribute payments and perhaps allow him to regain lost territories. The annals of Chinese history warned of the risks of helping one potential enemy to defeat another, but those lessons were lost on Huizong, who ordered his army to join in the Jurchen attack on Liao.

That decision proved doubly disastrous. First, imperial forces were repulsed in humiliating fashion by the Khitans. Then the Jurchens conquered the Khitans on their own and turned on the demoralized Chinese, sweeping across the border on horseback in 1126 and galloping toward Kaifeng. As the invading forces drew near, Huizong abdicated in favor of his eldest son, Qinzong. Some claimed that the abdication had been foreshadowed a year earlier when a fox escaped from the royal pleasure park and settled on Huizong's throne in his absence—a bad omen indeed.

Qinzong tried to avert disaster by offering ransom to the Jurchens, but he later reneged on the deal and they renewed their siege. In 1127 the Jurchens stormed the city and rounded up the imperial retinue—including Qinzong and his father, Huizong; their respective empresses, Zhu and Zheng; dozens of their secondary wives and relatives; and some 3,000 imperial retainers and officials. To prevent those captives from being re-claimed by Chinese forces, the Jurchens herded them northward on a brutal trek. Women close to the emperor and his father were seized by their captors as wives or slaves, and Qinzong's own empress, Zhu, became the target of a Jurchen officer who tried to shame him into handing her over. "Why are you so stingy about sharing the empress with another man?" he asked. "It's heaven's retribution that you've become what you are today. You deserve it."

Empress Zhu died several weeks later, and her body was tossed away unceremoniously in a straw mat. Some time later Huizong's empress, Zheng, fell desperately ill and could no longer walk. Rather than leave her alone to perish by the side of the road, Qinzong lifted her onto his back and carried her, but she died the following morning. The two grieving emperors sur-

poor, leading to peasant uprisings in 1120 and 1121. People were losing faith in the Son of Heaven—and disaster loomed.

The agents of doom were the Jurchens, hard-riding hunters and herdsmen based to the north in Manchuria. By 1121, they had come close to defeating China's old adversaries, the Khitans. Huizong and his top advisers looked favorably on that development, for China was still paying an annual tribute of silver and silk to the Khitan state of Liao, as specified by a century-old peace treaty. A Jurchen victory, Huizong reasoned, would save

vived the trek, only to languish in captivity for the rest of their lives. Huizong soon went blind—a result, it was said, of weeping incessantly for his departed wife and for his own lost glory. He died in 1135, at the age of 53. To the end, he blamed his plight on others. The Song dynasty had been brought to ruin by "treacherous ministers," he told his son, who outlived him by some two decades. "There have been many subjugated rulers since ancient times. None of them suffered as miserably as I have."

Huizong's lament for the passing of the Song dynasty was premature, however. Unbeknown to him, his ninth son, Gaozong, had escaped the Jurchens, having been away on a government mission when the invaders sacked Kaifeng. Gaozong fled south to the burgeoning city of Hangzhou, where he rallied his forces and perpetuated his dynasty, known thereafter as the Southern Song. He was not the only member of the imperial family to elude captivity. In retaining authority, he received great help from a former empress named Meng, who had been ousted from the palace in humiliating fashion but who managed in the end to restore both her own dignity and the Song fortunes.

The daughter of a prominent army officer, Meng had been selected at the age of 16 from among 100 candidates to be bride and future empress to Huizong's predecessor, Zhezong, who had not yet taken the throne when he and Meng were married. She was not in fact chosen by Zhezong but by his strong-willed

Peasants clear a forest and stack up timber to facilitate a campaign by the army against China's troublesome northern foes in the year 1115. Although this particular campaign proved successful, fierce invaders called Jurchens swept down a decade or so later and conquered northern China.

grandmother and regent. After the old woman died, Zhezong became emperor, and his ardor for Meng cooled. He transferred his affections to another of his consorts, the alluring Liu, whose hold over him only increased when she bore him his first son and heir. Determined to supplant Meng as empress, Liu conspired with an influential palace eunuch to bring charges of witchcraft against her rival, using testimony obtained from palace retainers under torture. Despite her pleas of innocence, the empress was found guilty, deposed in favor of Liu, and exiled to a Daoist sanctuary.

Her banishment proved to be her salvation when the Jurchens overran Kaifeng. An old imperial outcast, Meng was ignored when others in the ruling family were rounded up and marched off. The Jurchens then installed as emperor in Kaifeng a puppet of theirs. Like an invalid who lacked the strength to rule on his own, that unpopular figurehead prevailed on Meng to serve as his regent to legitimize his regime. She soon discovered that Gaozong had survived, however, and acknowledged him as China's rightful emperor by stepping down as regent. The grateful Gaozong then had her spirited out of Kaifeng and welcomed her to his court.

In 1129 Gaozong suffered a defeat in his ongoing struggle with the Jurchens, and captains of his bodyguard turned against him, forcing him to abdicate in favor of his three-year-old son. The renegades asked Meng to serve as regent to the youngster and she reluctantly accepted, not to glorify herself but to protect the prince. Ultimately, Gaozong regained control of his forces, and Meng gladly yielded to him. Once again, she relinquished her regency, restoring the boy to his father's care and remaining at court as an honored figure. By the time Meng died in 1134, the future of the dynasty was assured. She had earned her place among the true guardians of China.

# RELIGION AND ETHICS

An ancient Chinese saying, "The three teachings flow into one," serves to illustrate the harmonious relationship that developed over time among China's great philosophical and religious traditions—Confucianism, Daoism, and Buddhism.

Confucianism, based on the teachings of the legendary sage Confucius, provided an ethical compass for Chinese social and government interactions for centuries. Set down in the fifth century BC, Confucianism stressed the importance of moral behavior, including respect for elders and strict rules of courtesy, and called for an individual to strive unceasingly for self-improvement. In contrast, Daoist philos-

ophy encouraged its practitioners to simply follow the flow of nature and be content. Based on the mystical writings of the renowned sages Laozi and Zhuangzi, Daoism eventually evolved into a fully organized communal religion. Unlike the indigenous traditions of Confucianism and Daoism, Buddhism was imported from India. Emphasizing the illusory nature of the material world, Buddhism's appeal was its promise of Enlightenment and salvation for the faithful.

By the time of the Song dynasty, all three of these traditions were interwoven into the lives of the Chinese people. Many families who followed Confucian ritual in their homes, for example, would also observe Buddhist holidays and festivals or ask a Daoist practitioner to exorcise an evil spirit. And in contrast to periods of Chinese history when either Buddhism or Daoism was favored by the regime in power, the religions coexisted peacefully in all social classes during the Song period.

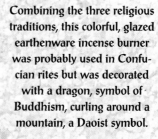

Combining the three religious traditions, this colorful, glazed earthenware incense burner was probably used in Confucian rites but was decorated with a dragon, symbol of Buddhism, curling around a mountain, a Daoist symbol.

The Daoist sage Laozi leans lovingly toward the infant Buddha, who squirms in the paternal embrace of Confucius in this silk painting representing the lack of conflict among the three traditions.

*"The Great Dao flows everywhere. . . .*
*All things depend on it for life,*
*and it does not turn away from them."*

A procession consisting of members of the Daoist hierarchy
(with tablets) and their attendants is depicted in this wall painting from the Yuan dynasty. Leading the way are the Jade
Emperor, ruler of nature *(center)*; his consort, the Empress of
Heaven *(left)*; and Laozi, legendary founder of Daoism *(right)*.

# FOLLOWING THE WAY

Daoism's main sacred text, the *Dao de jing,* called on humankind to follow the natural, cosmic flow of the universe, known as Dao, or "the Way." Humans, the text advised, were part of this natural flow and would be foolish to try to impose order upon it. Although this philosophy contradicted Confucianism, its adoption allowed the Chinese people to utilize tenets from either belief as life's circumstances dictated.

Getting closer to the natural world was the path to inner peace and balance in one's life, according to the Daoists. One should choose the simple over the complex and submission over resistance, with the goal of becoming "formless, desireless, without striving . . . content." Early adepts embraced simple diets and exercise and sometimes abandoned civi-lization entirely, living as hermits in forests or mountains. There, they believed, they could attain spiritual immortality as their bodies disintegrated and their souls were released into the universe.

By the second century AD, however, Daoists believed they could achieve detachment anywhere, and they began seeking immortality through the magic arts. In addition, Daoism appropriated elements of popular Chinese folk beliefs, and it took on the trappings of formalized religion, complete with temples, priests, and a bureaucratic hierarchy of celestial gods and mythical immortals. Priests were thought to possess supernatural powers, which enabled them not only to cure illness, exorcise demons, and invoke heavenly spirits, but also to predict the future.

Daoism was enduringly popular with the common people, and it vied with Buddhism for a hold on China's rulers. During the Song dynasty, Emperor Huizong converted many Buddhist monasteries to Daoist temples and compiled the first complete Daoist canon in Chinese history.

Reading ancient texts, a Daoist immortal sits nestled under a tree on this silver wine vessel. Daoists believed that wine brought out man's true nature, and the vessel's inscription reads, "Only those who know the joy of wine / Remain immortalized in this world when they die."

# THE SEARCH FOR ENLIGHTENMENT

"I teach only two things, O disciples, the fact of suffering and the possibility of escape from suffering." These words of the Buddha's referred to the suffering brought about by man's desires. The only hope of relief from that suffering, Buddha continued, was to attain a higher consciousness, which he called Enlightenment. That state could be achieved through compassionate behavior, meditation, and asceticism.

Founded by the Indian prince Siddhartha Gautama, Buddhism was an organized religion by the first century AD, when it was introduced into China by merchants arriving from India. It spread slowly at first, mainly among Chinese scholars and aristocrats, but by the early fourth century, its rituals, repetitive prayers, and pantheon of benevolent supernatural beings, such as Bodhisattvas and Luohans, had drawn in the common folk as well.

By the Tang dynasty, just before the Song period, thousands of Buddhist temples dotted the countryside, and its monasteries were filled with men and women who had forsaken society. Threatened by the power and wealth of the monasteries, the state dismantled many of them and confiscated their land. But Buddhism had too thoroughly permeated China to be eliminated.

The form of Buddhism that flourished in China during the Song dynasty was uniquely Chinese and split between two sects—Pure Land and Chan. The former offered salvation to all who invoked the name of Amitabha, the Buddha of compassion who presided over the paradise known as Pure Land. This sect appealed to a wide range of followers, particularly the poor. In contrast, Chan Buddhism (known as Zen in Japan) was an intellectual movement begun by Chinese monks. Popular among officials and merchants, this branch of Buddhism held that Enlightenment could only be experienced intuitively, as a sudden revelation that occurs after long periods of meditation and withdrawal from the material world.

Captured at the moment of his Enlightenment, a Chan Buddhist priest literally strains to embrace the sudden flash of insight from which he has achieved total understanding of the universe.

Five Buddhist guardian saints known as Luohans descend from the clouds to receive offerings from devotees and to enjoy a sumptuous feast in this 12th-century silk painting.

Supplicants bearing incense kneel at the feet of the Bodhisattva Guanyin, saint of compassion and mercy, who rescues souls from hell—depicted in the surrounding scenes—and leads them to salvation. Guanyin's mustache is a holdover from Indian Buddhism, which portrayed the being as male.

51

# CHAPTER TWO

# Resurgence in the South

Porters stagger under heavy loads and vendors cry out to pedestrians while bargemen caught in the canal's swirling current struggle to lower the mast of their boat and pass safely beneath Rainbow Bridge in Kaifeng. Such boisterous scenes were equally common in the southern city of Hangzhou, which replaced Kaifeng as the capital of the Song dynasty in the 12th century.

 More than a half century before Emperor Gaozong fled south from occupied Kaifeng and revived the Song court in the city of Hangzhou, a gifted scholar-official named Su Shi sought his own refuge there. Unlike Gaozong's hasty flight from the northern invaders, Su Shi's departure in 1071 was a well-considered retreat—from a losing battle in Kaifeng with chief councilor Wang Anshi and his fellow reformers.

The reformers had already made one attempt to bring Su down, after Su sent a series of memorials to Emperor Shenzong condemning Wang's policies as well as his efforts to drive from office the censors who so forcefully denounced him. Rulers had long nurtured such sharp criticism by granting the censors "weighty powers," Su pointed out to the emperor. "Why? To ensure that treacherous officials are rooted out just as they sprout."

A talented writer and poet, Su was not one to mince words, and his stinging rhetoric earned him the hatred of Wang Anshi and his influential supporters. Su soon lost his post in Kaifeng as an imperial historian and found himself being investigated on dubious charges, including salt smuggling. The government jealously guarded its monopoly on salt, a highly prized preservative that brought in much-needed revenue. "Let them investigate all they want," Su wrote to a relative living in Sichuan. "I know they will only make fools of themselves."

Su Shi's career as a scholar-official had begun brightly enough when he and his younger brother, Su Che, had passed the civil service examinations in 1057. Su Shi finished second among the successful candidates that year, and his brother was not far behind. The impressed emperor reportedly proclaimed that in these brothers he had found two chief councilors for his descendants. But neither would ever fulfill that hope, because the older brother had one fatal flaw: He spoke the truth as he saw it, despite the consequences. "When I feel something is wrong, it is like finding a fly in my food," he once remarked. "I just have to spit it out."

Su Shi's outspokenness made him a target of the reformers a dozen years later, but as he predicted, the charges against him were dismissed. Like others who ran afoul of the formidable Wang Anshi, however, he decided that it was time to leave Kaifeng. He asked for a provincial post and got one—as vice prefect of Hangzhou. It was not much of a job for a man of his talents. Yet Su Shi was perhaps more fortunate than he knew in this first encounter with the reformers, for he walked away from the confrontation without undergoing a trial. He would not be so lucky the next time.

His new post, Hangzhou, would become the glittering capital of the Southern Song in the following century, but when he arrived there in 1071, it was only a small city. Yet its beautiful setting immediately captured his poet's heart. Forested mountains ringed the city on the north, west, and south. Between city and mountains lay the gleaming expanse of West Lake, constructed centuries earlier by damming the streams that ran down from the mountains. To the east the Zhe River rolled toward the open sea.

Guarding the city's vulnerable eastern flank was an outer rampart that had been built in the ninth century and was bordered by a huge moat, which was sealed by a floodgate at high tide. The city itself was entirely enclosed by 30-foot-high walls, raised in the seventh century and built of packed earth and stone. People entering Hangzhou

Flooded rice paddies reflect a spectacular backdrop of mountains in southern China. The region's fertile landscape, crisscrossed with rivers and canals, proved ideal for farming as well as for trading, and it nurtured the golden age of the Southern Song.

From his house and garden high on Phoenix Hill, at the south end of town where the government officials lived, Su Shi could admire the panorama below. To one side lay the river, crowded with shipping; to the other lay the lake, nine miles around and nine feet deep. Its waters reflected the cloud-swathed mountains and their pine forests, where here and there rose the pagodas and roofs of the town's numerous temples. It was a heavenly view. As a visitor wrote a century later, "Green mountains surround on all sides the still waters of the lake. Pavilions and towers in hues of gold and azure rise here and there. One would say, a landscape composed by a painter. Only towards the east, where there are no hills, does the land open out, and there sparkle, like fishes' scales, the bright colored tiles of a thousand roofs."

Su Shi's official duties were not too arduous, leaving him time to sample the pleasures of the town and countryside. He mingled with people from all walks of life, reveling in the joys of good food, drink, and companionship and earning praise for his poetry. The city had long been a center for Buddhist scholarship and worship, and he also journeyed up into the surrounding hills to visit Hangzhou's monasteries. Studying with its masters, he acquired the Buddhist belief in a single unity that permeates all things. In meditating, he learned to empty his mind of earthly attachments so as to perceive this oneness. A world seen this way was regarded with infinite compassion. Su Shi, already sympathetic to those in need, learned from his mentors that compassion alone was not enough; to purify himself, he had to perform good works—in particular, works that resulted in the saving of life. True to that belief, he would labor diligently throughout his career to ease the lot of the thousands of peasants who came under his care.

Su Shi's first stay at Hangzhou was brief, and it would be many years before he returned—years of tribulation and exile occasioned by his ongoing conflict with the reformers, whose notions of how to help China's peasantry differed markedly from

passed through one of 13 arched and towered road gates or five water gates, for the canals that flowed through the town.

The city within must have looked provincial to Su Shi compared with the capital he left behind. The main avenue through the center of Hangzhou was perhaps 60 yards wide—no match for the stunning Imperial Way at Kaifeng, some 300 yards across. But Hangzhou had its own special charms. Stone bridges spanned the narrow canals, which were covered with blossoming lotus; shaded by plum, peach, pear, and apricot trees; and flanked by busy arcades where merchants plied their wares.

his own. Ultimately, he would regain favor and find his way back to Hangzhou as a prominent official, helping to make it the great city later embraced by the Southern Song as their capital. In his own time, he would never be a dominant figure like his nemesis, Wang Anshi. But Su Shi was a harbinger of things to come—a China that would endure dissension and defeat and emerge to reach fresh heights of accomplishment.

In 1074, having completed his stint in Hangzhou, Su Shi bid a reluctant farewell to the city and took up a new post in Mizhou, situated in the northeastern province of Shandong. There he protested bitterly yet ineffectually against the government's continuing salt monopoly, which often priced this precious resource beyond the peasants' means. Balancing work with pleasure, he had a tower erected on the city wall, where he could view the landscape and entertain.

At his next position, Su oversaw work on a remarkable flood-control project along the Yellow River, living amid the construction all the while. While he was serving there, he took the unusual step of providing a physician for inmates of the local prisons, which were crammed with people who had been detained for smuggling salt or failing to pay their debts. Su Shi was among those who criticized Wang Anshi's troubled Green Sprouts program—which offered farmers loans at interest rates lower than those exacted by private lenders—on the grounds that it was driving people deeper into debt by saddling them with loans they did not want or could not handle.

Su Shi even went so far as to criticize that program in verse. Under Green Sprouts, he wrote, farmers accompanied by their sons had to travel to town in the spring to apply for loans, and then return in the fall to repay them. Government officials frequently delayed the applicants in town for weeks. When the farmers finally did receive their loans, government wine shops would stage elaborate entertainments that included gambling, in order to siphon off some of the money. The only thing a farmer had to show for his efforts when he returned home, Su Shi claimed, was a son who had lost a lot of money and had taken on some city polish:

> *With bramble staff and bundles of cooked rice he hurried off,*
> *Yet copper coins passed through his hands in a flash.*
> *What he's won is a son whose accent has improved,*
> *More than half the year they've spent in town!*

Plainly, Su's earlier troubles in Kaifeng had not taught him to watch his words. As he put it, poems poured out of him "like the sailing of clouds or the flowing of water," and he made no effort to stem the flow or filter out what others might consider impure thoughts. Some of his verses celebrated the world's beauty and life's joys, but others railed against those in power and the pain and suffering he blamed on their misdeeds. Sometimes obliquely, sometimes more clearly, Su criticized the reform policies. His fame as a poet grew, as did the demand for his verses. He sent poems in his letters to friends and family; he carved inscriptions on stones; he painted verses in his own beautiful hand on courtesans' fans and shawls. People collected his work and printed the collections, which circulated to Kaifeng, where they provoked great interest—and indignation.

"Su Shi's writing is the most marvelous in the world," a close friend observed. "His only shortcoming is that he likes to rebuke people." Rebuke them he did. The poet mercilessly lampooned Wang Anshi, a man of deep convictions, as the philosopher of the "Three Not-Worths," who believed that "God's anger is not worth fearing, public opinion is not worth respecting, and the tradition of the ancestors is not worth keeping." The poet compared Wang's followers to "monkeys given baths and caps to look like human beings," as well as to crows feeding on rotten meat; he likened their conversation to the croaking of frogs and the buzzing of cicadas.

A group of divine beings known as Luohans wash their clothes in a mountain stream, watched by a fierce-faced demon who has been tamed by the wisdom of these Buddhist saints. The Chinese worshiped these holy men who had attained spiritual enlightenment, and the many monasteries around Hangzhou displayed images of Luohans as well as Buddhas.

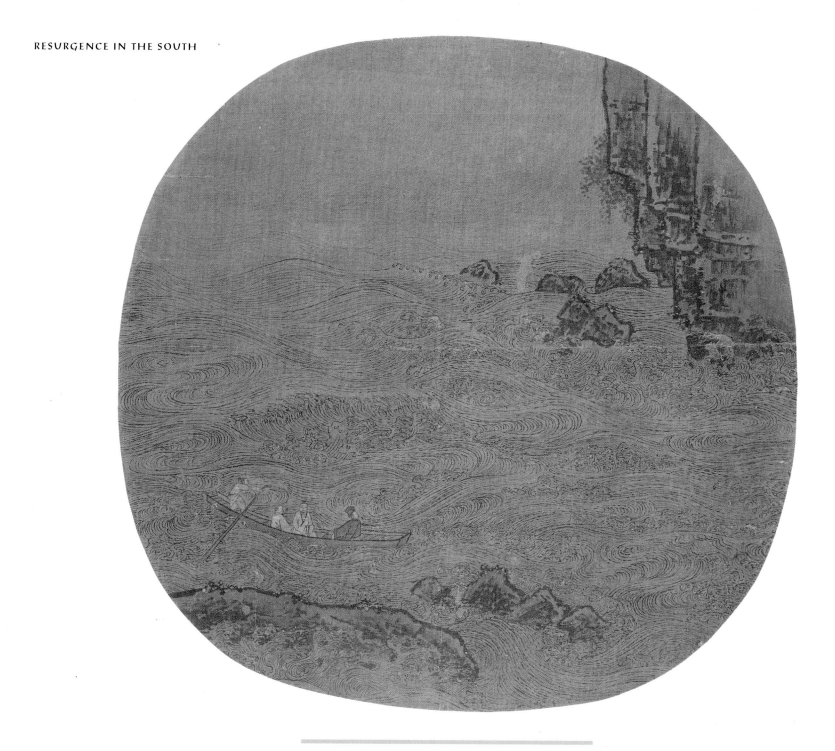

In a painting originally mounted on a fan, poet Su Shi and companions ride the roiling waters of the Yangzi River. The exhilarating trip, taken while Su was living in exile in a small village along the Yangzi, inspired him to write, "We soared freely as if we had left the world behind, sprouting wings and rising aloft like immortals."

Many of the reformers he mocked remained in high positions after Wang himself retired from office in 1076, and they found all this hard to stomach. By 1079 they had had their fill. Four volumes of Su's poems were in print, and ridicule from a famous poet was doing nothing to ease the tensions at court. "Today our institutions are not yet complete and customs not yet unified," wrote one of the imperial censors, now firmly allied with the reformers. "This is precisely the moment we should make clear to the empire the basis of imperial reward and punishment. Faced with such a vile person as Shi, can we simply desist and not take action?" The poet would have to pay for his literary outbursts.

On July 28, 1079, Su Shi, now serving as prefect of the southern town of Huzhou, peered outside his office to find a court envoy, dressed in formal gown, and two armed guards from the Censorate waiting in the courtyard. Such a delegation from the capital of Kaifeng could mean only that Su was in profound trouble. With pounding heart, he donned his own official gown and, accompanied by his deputy, walked outside.

"I know I have done many things to anger the court," Su Shi confessed to the envoy. "I don't mind dying, but please allow me to go home to say farewell to my family."

"It is not so bad as that," the official replied, but there was no real reassurance in his voice.

One of the guards stepped forward and handed Su's deputy a document, which stripped Su of his office and ordered him to appear in Kaifeng to face criminal charges. The charges included slandering the court—and worse, the emperor—and arousing unrest among the people. Those were capital crimes, and if found guilty, Su Shi could pay with his life.

News of the arrest spread through Huzhou, and weeping family members and townspeople gathered to bid the popular prefect good-bye. Traveling north toward Kaifeng with his guards, the prisoner pondered his uncertain future. As the miles passed, dread weighed ever more heavily upon him, and by the time the party reached the Yangzi River, he felt the urge to drown himself in its waters. "But the soldiers guarded me closely," he later confided to a friend, and suicide was impossible.

The investigation and trial in Kaifeng lasted four long months. Agents ransacked his family's belongings for subversive poems. (Angry at the poet's indiscretion, family members then burned most of the manuscripts that were left.) Inscriptions on public monuments were scrutinized, and letters he had sent to friends were confiscated. After weeks of interrogation about his writings, Su Shi broke down and admitted to maligning members of the court and their programs, but not with any disloyal intent toward the emperor. "I expressed my disapproval of the New Policies in poetry," he later explained, "hoping to change the emperor's mind."

Su Shi was fortunate in having among his defenders prominent government officials, including his devoted younger brother—who offered to take his place in punishment—and Wang Anshi's younger brother. That a troublemaker like Su still had friends in high places was proof that dissenting opinions had not been entirely suppressed in the capital. Indeed, few officials on either side of this fierce debate were entirely without scruples—or so caught up in the conflict that they wanted to see their opponents dead. In the end, Su Shi was not executed. Instead, he was exiled, sentenced to spend the rest of his days in a poor village along the middle Yangzi River. In addition, his brother was demoted and sent to run a government wine shop located in southern China.

Confined to the countryside, his salary cut off, Su struggled to support his family with his meager savings. By the second year of his exile, he reported, "my money was running out." Learning of his plight, a friend convinced the district government to grant Su 10 acres on the eastern slope of a mountain above the village. Always sympathetic to the farmers, the poet would now learn

# GHOSTS AND GODS

Chinese folk religion focused not on doctrine but on such practical concerns as health, fortune, and fertility. Gods, spirits, and ghosts of every description inhabited the universe, and people sought blessings from dragons and other benevolent supernatural beings while trying to appease demons or drive them away.

The Chinese worshiped household deities to protect their families and nature spirits to favorably influence the world around them. They built shrines not only to the heavenly gods associated with Buddhism and Daoism but also to earthly saints, sages, and heroes—including their esteemed ancestors, who, if not properly propitiated with offerings, might become "hungry ghosts," scavenging in graveyards and preying upon the living.

Holidays and festivals combined superstition with celebration and were occasions for individual and communal rituals. The most important of these was New Year's,

To drive out evil spirits, 12 village elders wearing outlandish hats beat drums, sound clappers, and ring bells during an exorcism dance.

which occurred a month or more after the winter solstice. Beforehand, families prepared special vegetable and soybean dishes for the god of the hearth so that he would report favorably on their conduct during his annual visit to heaven. People hung images of Zhong Kui, a legendary demon queller, over their doors to keep demons out, and pharmacists distributed amulets to ward off evil spirits. Once these protective measures had been observed, it was safe to celebrate.

Worn around the waist, this talisman offered its owner the protection of two star gods as well as the promise of magical powers and forgiveness of sins.

Passengers crowd the deck of an elaborate dragon boat as it competes in the annual race during the Dragon Boat Festival. According to tradition, dragons were helpful water spirits, and vessels in their image would frighten away ghosts and demons.

about their lives from a different vantage point—behind a plow. Wisely, he sought help from the local farmers in his daunting new enterprise, as he recorded in a poem about planting wheat:

*It's less than a month since I did the sowing,*
*Even now the tilled soil shows some green.*
*An old farmer came and told me,*
*'Don't let the sprouts get thick with leaves;*
*If you want ample noodles and dumplings,*
*Let sheep and oxen in to graze.'*
*I bow twice in thanks for this frank advice,*
*When my stomach's full, I won't forget him.*

Exile had not forced Su to put down his pen. He had been forbidden to write on government affairs, but he continued to express himself on a range of scholarly subjects and on village life. One of his delights at his mountainside home was a pavilion called the Snow Hall, whose walls he painted with winter scenes. He called himself Recluse of the Eastern Slope and came to be known as Su Dongpo (Eastern Slope). In his banishment, he found a certain peace. After all, he had been born in Sichuan, along the upper Yangzi River, and he felt more at home here than in the capital. His opponents had done him a favor of sorts by exiling him to the south, a region that encompassed the land along the Yangzi River and everything below it. While Kaifeng remained rooted in the past, this was the land of China's future.

Unlike Su Shi, many Chinese of the ruling class would have found no consolation in a banishment from Kaifeng to southern China. For them, China's heart beat in the north, on the vast plains of the Yellow River, birthplace of their ancient civilization. Dead emperors of old dynasties, ancestors of their own, lay buried on those wind-swept plains. Yet southern China was a golden territory, crisscrossed by a multitude of rivers and canals. The southeast in particular was warm, lush, and fertile. Rice—

the grain with a higher yield per acre than any other—flourished in this region's paddies, which had fed the north for centuries.

Those centuries had seen far-reaching developments in China, many of which spurred advances in the well-watered south rather than in the dry north. Southern farmers had a plow adapted for turning paddy mud that required only one ox or water buffalo, not the four needed on dry land. The paddies themselves were carefully shaped and irrigated through the use of dams, dikes, and sluice gates. By such means, farmers changed the shape of the southeast coast, holding back the salt tide and rerouting rivers to make polders: lowland tracts of farmland protected by dikes. At the same time, they conquered the hills by building reservoirs and terraces. And from what is now Vietnam, China imported in the 11th century new rice seed that could be grown in poor soil and was drought resistant and quick ripening.

The government, through its circulating officials, did everything possible to spread agricultural advances throughout China. That included painting "how-to" murals on walls to instruct illiterate farmers. Using woodblock printing, invented in the ninth century, officials also printed and circulated illustrated books offering simple instruction. By Su Shi's time, all this effort had yielded major benefits. Selective breeding of grain had produced rice for various soils, climates, and seasons, allowing for at least two harvests a year in the prime rice-growing regions of southern China—one in early summer and another in the fall.

Although the peasants endured great hardship and were prey to devastating floods and droughts, the dramatic advances in agriculture fostered a rapid increase in population—from little more than 50 million in the 10th century to 100 million by the 13th century—and enabled people to produce food for trade as well as for subsistence. Farmers grew for sale such items as lychees, oranges, and cane sugar in the sultry province of Fujian on the southeast coast, for example, or tea in the damp

Holding a stick with a bird tethered to it, a barefoot boy tends a lumbering water buffalo in the countryside. Among the Chinese, it was the children's job to take care of such domesticated beasts, which were often owned communally by several families.

hills of Sichuan. For trade, they also cultivated hemp, cotton, mulberry trees for silkworms, and other trees for timber or lacquer. And though most Chinese worked in the fields, increasing numbers toiled in industries like fabric weaving, papermaking, ceramics, and printing.

To carry goods from one region to another, the Chinese maintained a vast network of arteries linking far-flung villages and towns. Although public works crews toiled mightily on China's remarkable road system, they labored even harder to dredge and extend the waterways—not simply to reduce the risk of flooding but also to provide merchants with water transport that was 30 to 40 percent cheaper than conveying goods by road. The great rivers of China were linked by well-tended canals—notably the Grand Canal, which by late Song times extended from the Yellow River in the north to Hangzhou in the south.

In transportation as in agriculture, southern China with its numerous waterways had an advantage over the north. Village markets sprang up at the confluence of those waterways. Some families lived in boats on the water, and people made their living by carrying goods around the impassable stretches of rivers or by poling ships through dangerous gorges. Such expert watermen enabled Su Shi to travel safely through the Three Gorges of the Yangzi in Sichuan when he was young, riding down rapids past bluffs hundreds of feet high. The poet later evoked that thrilling journey in verse:

> *The winds bellowed through the cliffs,*
> *And the clouds spewed forth from the caves . . .*
> *Falling cataracts spread a shower of snowy mist,*
> *And strange rocks sped past like horses in fright.*

International trade flourished as well. In earlier times, the Chinese had traded extensively by caravan with lands to their north and west. But now hostile powers along the northern and western borders restricted that overland commerce, and the Chinese responded by developing the greatest merchant fleet in the world, with huge oceangoing ships called junks that ranged as far as the Persian Gulf.

The imperial government cashed in on trade and commerce in every possible way. It had to, for its direct taxes, such as those on grain, were not enough to meet its own expenses and maintain the vast armies protecting its threatened borders. Even during hostilities, Song officials maintained trading posts in the

An overseer, protected from the sun by a parasol, directs a small group of workers as they cut and bundle ripened stalks of rice in a field drained for harvest. The Song government taught farming methods using step-by-step illustrations such as this one.

north. China needed horses, and horsemen to the north who were not too busy raiding the Chinese gladly traded with them, providing mounts in exchange for grain, silk, tea, and paper. The government's monopolies in salt, tea, alcohol, and incense brought in much-needed revenues as well.

The imperial treasury received no help from the big landowning families, who managed to avoid paying taxes on the proceeds of their vast estates, which sometimes encompassed several villages. Instead, it was their tenants and the independent small farmers, graded from one to five according to how much land they owned, who paid—and paid. They owed rents on land, interest on loans, taxes on produce, taxes on salt, taxes on their most mundane purchases. They could barely get by, even with good harvests. Bad ones meant crushing debts, loss of land, and famine.

Desperate poverty led to desperate measures. While working his own farm, Su Shi observed among his neighbors the grim practice—common in the countryside—known as bathing the infant. "The poor farmers as a rule raise only two sons and one daughter and kill babies at birth beyond this number," he wrote. "A baby is often killed at birth by drowning in cold water, but in order to do this the baby's parents have to close their eyes and avert their faces." Officials tried to halt infanticide by threatening to enforce the law against the killing of descendants or by arranging for adoptions, but these were frail measures in the face of poverty so overwhelming that even one more mouth to feed was a catastrophe. Infanticide remained the custom in the country; in the city, people abandoned their unwanted babies on the streets.

When limiting the size of the family was not

The Chinese terrorized their enemies by camouflaging the paddle wheels of their boats so that they appeared to move by magic.

River junks crowd a busy section of the Yellow River near Kaifeng (*left*). Below, wind fills the accordion-like sails of a seagoing junk, whose builders adorned its bow with a circular eye to help it "see" across the ocean.

# MASTERING THE WATERWAYS

Over the centuries, the Chinese built a range of boats and ships to ply their rivers and strike out across the ocean. Vessels known as junks were powered by the wind, which was trapped with great efficiency in sails stiffened by horizontal bamboo battens. Those same sails were easily trimmed in the fierce storms that raged in the South China Sea by being contracted like an accordion. Watertight bulkheads—separate compartments in the hold—meant that junks, unlike Western ships of the era, could stay afloat even when they had sprung a leak. During the Song period, Chinese traders were able to sail their hardy ships to ports as far away as Africa.

Ships and boats were steered with a single stern-mounted rudder that could be raised or lowered, an advantage in the shallow waters of rivers and canals. To transport grain and other goods through these inland waterways, they used smaller vessels propelled by sails or by a long-handled sculling oar pushed, rather than pulled, by standing oarsmen. One Chinese dictionary described the oar as "the thing on the boat's sides which is to be managed by strong muscles before the boat moves." Muscle power also drove the paddle wheels that propelled the empire's deadly "flying tiger warships" into battle.

enough, poor workers could sell themselves or their children into bondage, as one unfortunate stonemason did. Unable to feed his family, he signed a contract by which he sold his son to a relation for 200 bushels of wheat and 200 bushels of millet, with the option to repurchase the boy after six years for the same price. Another unpleasant possibility, for those who lost their land, was to hire out as agricultural laborers from February to October. The pay was eight bushels of grain a month, clothing for spring and summer, and a pair of leather shoes. For that the laborer had to work "without stopping from morning to evening." If he missed a day's work for any reason during the harvest or other busy times, he forfeited nearly one-half of his monthly grain payment.

The landless also went to work in factories. Peasants displaced from the rice fields of southern China might toil there in one of the many workshops devoted not only to lighter industries like ceramics, silk production, and papermaking, but also to hotter and heavier tasks like smelting iron. A villainous 12th-century industrialist named Wang Ge fueled his ironworks with charcoal produced by local farmers working in the off-season at a forested mountain he owned. An extortionist determined to dominate his region, Wang raised a rebellion against the local government, using his hapless foundry workers as a private army. When they in turn rebelled against him, Wang was caught by the authorities and executed. What happened to the workers is not recorded.

Worst of all, perhaps, were the government mines and saltworks, situated along the southeast coast and in the Huai River valley to the north. In that valley, 280,000 families—at least a million people—toiled on starvation wages, producing salt by

## SPINNERS OF SILK

The beautiful robes worn by the wealthy were the products of an ancient Chinese process that exploited the talents of one of nature's own spinners—the silkworm. In the 13th-century scroll above, painted on silk, a man picks mulberry leaves *(top right),* to be spread onto trays bearing newly hatched worms *(bottom right).*

Once the voracious leaf eaters have gorged on mulberry for a month and fattened, they will spin cocoons made of delicate strands of silken thread. Workers pack newly spun cocoons tightly into baskets *(bottom left)* to suffocate the developing insects inside before they can turn into moths and burst through the cocoons, ruining the valuable silk fibers.

such backbreaking means as flooding fields with seawater, allowing it to dry in the sun, scraping off the salt crystals, forming a brine from them, and then percolating the brine in huge vats until pure salt appeared. This grueling work was little better than slave labor. The only escape was to join the countless thousands fleeing to the great cities of the Yangzi basin, cities such as Nanjing, Huzhou, Suzhou, and Hangzhou.

Like many others, Su Shi too eventually left the countryside for the burgeoning city of Hangzhou, but not before making an unwelcome detour back to Kaifeng. He was recalled from exile to Kaifeng in 1085, when Emperor Shenzong, the patron of the reformers, died, and his mother, the empress dowager, brought conservatives back into power. Unlike many of his colleagues, Su was not happy to be returning to Kaifeng, with its partisan squabbles. This time it was his fellow conservatives that Su clashed with, for he knew more than most about the problems facing the poor and believed that one of Wang Anshi's policies—paid labor for public works—benefited the peasants and was worth saving. Weary of the wrangling and still in the empress dowager's favor, he asked for an assignment far from the capital. To his delight, he was appointed to a commanding position in the same beloved city where he had earlier served as vice prefect.

Approaching the whitewashed brick and earth ramparts of Hangzhou in 1089, Su Shi must have wondered if it would live up to his fond memories. The city, after all, had been his home in happier days, long before his arrest and exile. Would it welcome and inspire him as it had before?

To his relief, he found life in Hangzhou's streets little changed. There were restaurants, teahouses, and wine shops—the city was famous for its drinking—to suit every taste and pocketbook. The streets were busy and the shops open until 2:00 a.m., when drumbeats signaled the fourth of the night's five watches and people headed home. During festivals, however, the place was awake all night. An itinerant Japanese monk saw the town on such a night, during the Feast of Lanterns in February 1072. Every shop, he noted, hung out lamps of green or red glass; every doorway was adorned with embroideries or strings of jade beads; peddlers sold cooked food as well as tea by the cup; there were street dancers, magicians, acrobats, and singers with zithers and flutes.

Out on West Lake, elaborate pleasure boats drifted to and fro in its waters, steered by boatmen in distinctive yellow turbans. Some of these boats were floating restaurants: "The sound of chopping fish comes from the bow / And the fragrance of cooking rice issues from the stern," wrote Su Shi after a pleasant evening on one. Some of his outings were grand affairs—wine-and-supper parties for him and his fellow scholar-officials, with entertainment provided by Hangzhou's famed singing women.

## FOOD AND DRINK FOR ALL

The people of Hangzhou are merchants and sellers of food and drink," one Song writer pronounced, and another observed that no fewer than 234 tasty dishes could be found in the various eating establishments. Agricultural advances and a booming trade network in south China produced a veritable cornucopia in Hangzhou's outdoor markets. Rice, the most important item in the local diet, came in many varieties, including yellow rice, red lotus-seed rice, and fragrant rice. Pork, lamb, fish, partridge, quail, chicken, goose, and duck could all be found in the vendors' stalls.

Shoppers also made their selections from more than 30 kinds of vegetables, 17 types of beans, and a tempting array of exotic fruits. Tea, a luxury item at the beginning of the Song dynasty in the 10th century, had now become an everyday item for those of all ranks, and Hangzhou tea merchants did a booming business, thus benefiting the government, which monopolized the tea trade and supplied the merchants.

Like their descendants in modern times, the Chinese in the Song period divided foods into two cate-

gories: grains and "vegetables"–the latter meaning any food other than grain, including fish, fowl, and meat. Except during festivals, the Chinese considered the grain, not the vegetable, to be the main ingredient of most meals. Regardless of financial circumstances, the staples of the diet were basically the same for the rich and the poor, the difference lying in the quantity and quality of the food consumed.

People ate three meals a day. For many, breakfast, eaten around dawn, might consist of steamed cakes, fried puff-pastry shreds, and twice-seasoned soup. At noon people ate similar fare. Dinner was the most substantial meal, likely comprising more than one course. Cooks prepared most of their food in woks, braziers, and steamers, all of which used a minimum of fuel, always in short supply in China. Place settings included spoons, chopsticks, and bowls.

Although much cooking went on at home, eating

On a crowded city street, diners enjoy a leisurely meal on the balcony of a two-story restaurant while shoppers of all classes mingle at stalls and shops offering everything from food to weapons.

establishments catering to all social levels and tastes abounded in Hangzhou. Laborers with little money or those in a hurry bought a quick meal at flimsily constructed shops specializing in noodles or soup but serving no wine. People with more means and time patronized the restaurants, referred to as tea- and wine houses. Within the restaurants' sturdier walls, a man could buy both food and drink—and pay for the services of a prostitute as well. In the finer establishments, prostitute quarters adjoined the restaurant so the pleasures of sex could be added to a dining experience that might last for two days.

Diners had as much choice in wine as they did in food. Some 50 varieties of wine, made with rice rather than grapes, could be found in China. Renowned consumers of alcohol, Hangzhou residents condemned those who indulged in one quick drink and then went on their way. A 13th-century writer cautioned his readers against patronizing the capital's small retail wine shops: "To go drinking in such a place is called 'hitting the cup,' meaning that a person drinks only one cup; it is therefore not the most respectable place

and is unfit for polite company." Public drunkenness was such a common occurrence that balustrades had to be constructed along the canals to prevent revelers from falling into the water. Far from being condemned, such a state of inebriation was viewed by many as a way of identifying with the universe and experiencing a sense of power.

While servants prepare tea *(foreground)*, a group of scholars relaxes around a banquet table set with bowls for tea and ewers holding an equally important beverage—wine.

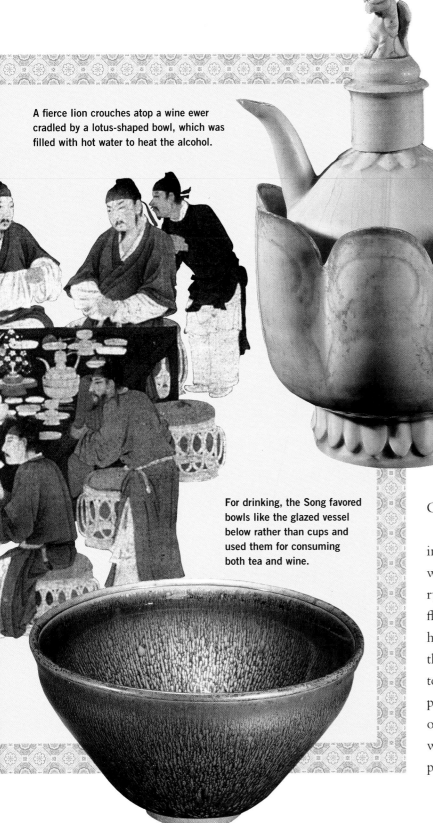

A fierce lion crouches atop a wine ewer cradled by a lotus-shaped bowl, which was filled with hot water to heat the alcohol.

For drinking, the Song favored bowls like the glazed vessel below rather than cups and used them for consuming both tea and wine.

Such singing women ranged from the hordes of poor prostitutes called "flowers," who gathered in the shopping arcades, to fancier girls in the taverns to exclusive courtesans. The most admired—and most richly rewarded—of those courtesans were small and slender, in the preferred style. They wore a pale foundation to lighten their complexion, tinged their cheeks with rouge, and painted their nails with pink balsam leaves crushed in alum. Their black hair was pulled back into great chignons and studded with silver, gold, and ivory combs.

Like the geisha of Japan, such courtesans enhanced their beauty with social graces. They were indeed singing girls and musicians, and some were talented poets as well. Their plaintive love songs had lilting lyrics and complex rhyme schemes. Su applied that style to all kinds of poems—love songs, drinking songs, laments, philosophical reflections. Inspired by the city and its seductive strains, he freed Chinese poetry from old, artificial modes, giving it new life.

Su Shi helped to preserve the charms of Hangzhou by clearing beautiful West Lake of the weeds that were choking it. This was a serious matter, for aside from inspiring pleasure and poetry the lake also provided fresh water for irrigating the fields, for flushing the Hangzhou canals, and for drinking. As vice prefect, he would have been unable to do much about the problem, but this time around, he was in a position to take action. He wrote to the empress dowager, asking for money to fund a reclamation project and warning that unless something was done soon, not only would the townspeople be hurt but the fish would suffer as well. Whether moved more by the plight of the people or the predicament of the fish, she granted his request. He immediately set to work clearing the weeds and silt. Ingeniously, he used the dredged-up muck to build a dike that created a sheltered pond along one side of the lake. Planted with willows, the embankment became a promenade for the townspeople, with six arched bridges and nine pavilions.

To protect the city's water supply, Su replaced Hangzhou's crumbling system of bamboo pipes with clay pipes, which funneled water from West Lake to reservoirs on the city's northwest side. From there water could be carried through the city by porters. He also worked to stave off starvation in 1089, when winter and spring flooding followed by summer drought guaranteed that the rice harvest in the region would fail. Customarily, officials waited for famine to occur and then dispensed rice as charity. But Su was not content with that remedy, for there was never enough

peace," he wrote. "It is not necessary to philosophize about the vicissitudes of human life. . . . I can just imagine myself to be a scholar candidate from Huizhou who has failed in the examinations and decides to live in his hometown for life."

In exile, he continued to work at public projects, soliciting donations and making his own contribution for a bridge across a dangerous stretch of water where people in small boats had been dying in the crossing for years; arranging for the burial of paupers' scattered corpses; and building barracks for government troops. He worked anonymously, since he was in disgrace. "Knowing that you are fond of doing good works, I now tell you this plan in secret," he wrote to a wealthy friend about a charitable scheme. "But you must not let anyone know it originated with me!"

By one account, the head of the reform

## "Scholars feel disgraced . . . when they cannot recite his poems in company."

government rice to stop starvation and the charitable distribution led to corruption, theft, and riots. Despite considerable opposition from other officials and indifference in Kaifeng, he saw to it that more rice was imported to the local market, thus keeping the price low and enabling people to stock up before the famine hit.

The people of Hangzhou and the surrounding region were grateful for Su's efforts, but neither his exemplary work there nor his good efforts in subsequent assignments saved him from retribution after the empress dowager died in 1093. Control of the government passed to her grandson, Zhezong, a supporter of the reformers. Within a year, Su was exiled once more, this time to subtropical Huizhou on the southeast coast. He found solace in the company of friends and family, however. "I feel quite at

party, upon learning that the poet was comfortable and happy, exiled him farther, to the semisavage island of Hainan, off the south coast, where he lived in reflective poverty with his youngest son. Not until 1100, when Emperor Zhezong died, was Su Shi recalled from exile. Now in his sixties, he died on the trip back.

Within a year of his death, his books were banned—which did nothing to reduce their appeal but simply drove the price up. As one writer put it, "Scholars feel disgraced and are considered uncultured when they cannot recite his poems in company." In time, Su Shi was restored posthumously to favor, and members of the imperial household joined in bidding for his manuscripts.

Such was his fame that when the Jurchens swept down from the north and seized Kaifeng in 1126, they claimed some of his

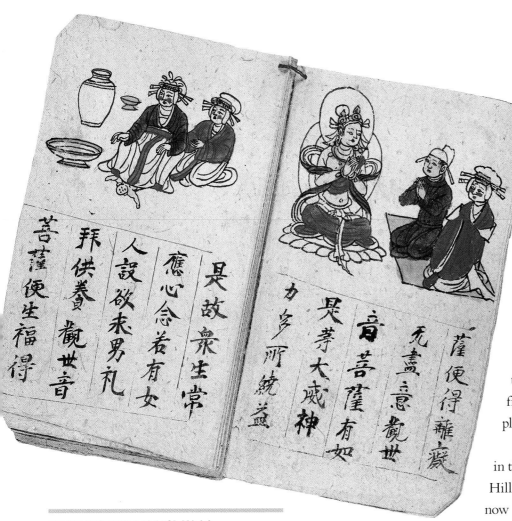

## CHILDBIRTH IN CHINA

In the illustrated Buddhist text above, a husband and wife kneel before the Bodhisattva Guanyin, praying for a child. The woman later gives birth with the aid of a midwife. Midwives generally assisted in delivering babies, but other experts might be summoned if complications arose.

According to one story, an acupuncturist saved a woman who had been in labor for a week. Believing the baby had grabbed the mother's intestine and would not let go, the acupuncturist felt the woman's belly to locate the tiny hand, then inserted a needle in the "tiger's mouth," the area between an infant's thumb and forefinger. The child's hand popped open, and he slid out through the birth canal.

manuscripts as booty, and they carried those prizes north along with thousands of imperial captives. Much of the rest of his work, however, ended up in the hands of Emperor Gaozong, who eluded the Jurchens and revived the Song dynasty in the south. His palace at Hangzhou was a fitting destination for the poet's writings, for the city had always considered Su Shi its own.

In the century after it became the Southern Song capital, Hangzhou grew into a city Su Shi would hardly have recognized, apart from its setting. Peasants from the countryside and immigrants from the north crammed it to bursting, and the surplus spilled over the ramparts into crowded suburbs. People lived cheek by jowl in those suburbs and in the lower, or northern, part of town, below Phoenix Hill. The main avenue, flanked by shady canals, was now called Imperial Way and provided a spacious route through the heart of Hangzhou. But the land on either side of it was packed with wooden and bamboo houses several stories high—unusual in China, where most buildings had just one level. Many of the dwellings had shops or workrooms on their ground floors and people living six or seven to a room on the floors above. "The houses are high and built close to each other," wrote a resident. "Their beams touch and their porches are continuous. There is not an inch of unoccupied ground anywhere."

Such quarters were a tinderbox. In 1132 a fire destroyed 13,000 houses, and another conflagration five years later flattened 10,000 more. In defense, Hangzhou organized fire watches. Lookouts in observation towers used flags by day and lanterns by night to indicate the location of a blaze so that squads of firefighters with buckets, ropes, hatchets, and scythes could be dispatched to quell the flames. To reinforce the regular firefighters, soldiers, whose normal duties were policing, were stationed at forts at the city gates. Even so, the lower town repeatedly had to rise phoenixlike from the ashes. In 1208 more than 58,000 houses fell to fire. The homeless were put up in monasteries around the town and issued cash and rice while they rebuilt.

Raging fires—and rampant thievery—inspired some enterprising residents to build warehouses of stone or other fireproof material, surrounded by canals and closely guarded, near the northeastern edge of town. Renting out safe warehousing space brought a handsome profit for a number of rich families, including the imperial one.

Except for the Imperial Way, which was reserved for the horses, sedan chairs, and long, curtained oxcarts of the rich, the streets were almost impassable. Those on foot had to weave around porters with burdens dangling from their poles as well as mules, donkeys, and small packhorses barely three feet high, called rabbit horses. Most people preferred to travel about the city by canals. Water taxis shared space with the endless streams of barges carrying rice—the city required 210 tons a day—to be unloaded at the Ricemarket Bridge and the Black Bridge in the northern suburbs.

The rice that flowed in was supplemented by local produce: green beans and soybeans, apricots and pears, and sundry other fruits and vegetables; goose and duck from West Lake; fish from fresh waters and

Customers crowd around the stalls of two competing scribes, who have taken their brushes, ink cakes, paper, and expertise in calligraphy to the streets to earn money. Hangzhou had street entrepreneurs of all sorts, including physiognomists, or face diviners, like the man standing under the sign at far right, who is telling a client's fortune by reading the shape of his face.

from the sea; game from the mountains; pigs and edible dogs from nearby farms. At the main pig market in the center of the city, off the Imperial Way, slaughtering with its attendant racket went on from past midnight until dawn. No oxen were slaughtered, for they were too valuable as draft animals to use as a food source.

The food filled local markets throughout the town and suburbs. Some 200 shops sold only salted fish. Fifteen big specialty markets, most of them outside the ramparts, sold fresh fish, crab, and vegetables. Other markets featured flowers, oranges, herbs, cloth, and books. Little shops in town offered groceries and necessities such as thread and lamp oil.

Despite the messy slaughterhouses and markets and the teeming crowds of poor people, local officials managed to keep the city clean. Well aware of the dangers of epidemics, governors had garbage removed regularly and barged to wasteland in the country. Each day, "pouring men" carted away the city's excrement, or night soil, to sell as manure for local gardens or vegetable plots in the eastern suburbs. With every New Year, there was a great tidying up of streets and canals. And the people here—unlike those in the cold,

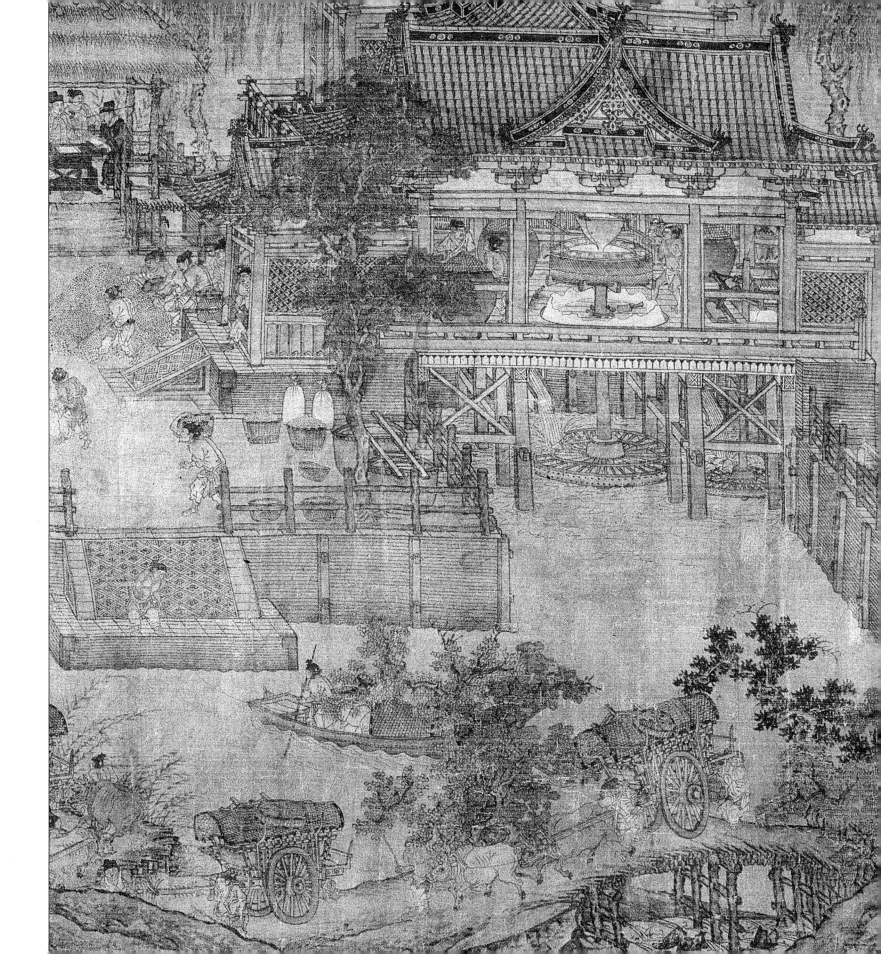

Using a millstone powered by a waterwheel, millers on a riverbank grind rice and other cereals to separate the edible grains from the husks. Farmers—who often delivered their harvests to mills in distant towns or cities by boat *(bottom left)*— were freed from the task of having to hull stalks manually, thus boosting crop production.

lice-ridden north—bathed daily at the bathhouses scattered about town, using a liquid soap made from peas and herbs. The locals believed cold water was healthy, but foreigners in Hangzhou could have their bathwater heated if they liked.

Not all in the city were tidy or clean living. The city had swarms of tattered beggars and brazen criminals—"those who in broad daylight seize foodstuffs and those who rob women of their jewelry," as one indignant observer wrote. "There are also cutpurses who cruise the streets at night, taking people's valuables and even causing injuries." Hangzhou had an organized underworld, with a Bureau of Beautiful People for fleecing rich young men, a Gambling Chest for card sharks, and another organization that specialized in creating crowd disturbances for the benefit of pickpockets and burglars. The army was supposed to police the streets, but the army itself was partly composed of criminals serving time in the ranks.

Those seeking to make an honest living did not have an easy time of it. The working poor scraped by as laborers, porters, and peddlers, whose distinctive cries echoed in the streets all day long and into the night. Some worked for shopkeepers, taking a 10 percent commission on sales; some got by on their own, going from door to door hawking cups of tea, noodles, roasted pork, sugarcane, candy shaped into little figures, or toys. Some joined the actors, storytellers, acrobats, jugglers, and puppeteers who enlivened the streets with their performances. Many residents, men and women both, worked as prostitutes in the markets or at the canals and bridges. The luckier of these were attached to taverns and bathhouses, just as the luckier members of other trades were attached to shops—for knife sharpening, pot mending, clearing out wells, or catering parties.

Hangzhou was known for conspicuous consumption, and scores of businesses served the wealthy. Most of the fine shops lay along the Imperial Way, where one could get rhinoceros horn from Bengal, ivory from India or Africa, and such luxuries as silk or porcelain from the vicinity of Hangzhou itself or other parts of China. One resident left a detailed guide to the best places to shop: for fine turbans, the Street of the Worn Cash Coin; for wicker cages, Ironware Lane; for ivory combs, a place called Fei's; for painted fans and folding fans (introduced from Korea in the 11th century), the Coal Bridge; for the best books, the tree-shaded stalls near the summerhouse at the Orange Tree Garden. The Pearl Market section of the Imperial Way drew shoppers interested in the city's own exquisite gold and silver hair ornaments.

One found a job at these places by applying to the guilds, which also handled the jobs offered on Phoenix Hill and the mountains around West Lake, where the great families lived. Many of those families were connected to the institutions that the Song had transferred from Kaifeng—the Imperial Palace, the National University, the Imperial Academy, the Military Academy, and the School of Medicine.

Their lavish homes were set around landscaped courtyards and offered respite from the noise and bustle of the town. The sloping roofs with their yellow or green tiles had upcurved edges, and terra-cotta dragons and phoenixes ornamented the ridges and eaves. The walls at either end were windowless brick, but the long sides under the overhanging eaves were more open, with doorways flanked by brick walls that were only about two feet high and surmounted by square latticework screens and windows glazed with oiled paper. The rooms inside remained shady and cool through Hangzhou's long, humid summer. In winter, people bundled up in fur and padded silk and warmed themselves as best they could over small braziers.

The wealthy decorated their homes with cool restraint. They favored graceful wooden tables and chairs, carved lacquered and curtained beds with padded silk coverlets, and hanging scrolls adorned with landscape paintings and calligraphy. Flowers brightened every room, skillfully arranged in the gray and white porcelain bowls and vases that Song potters made famous all over Asia. Hangzhou was known for its flowers—including the fragrant blossoms of assorted fruit trees, orchids, daphne, magnolia, 10 kinds of peony, and 70 kinds of chrysanthemum. Even the pets were stylish: Yellow and white cats known as lion cats could be bought

Beckoned by a theatrical troupe's drummer, an enraptured audience watches the antics of two puppets, manipulated by puppeteers hidden within a portable stage *(right)*. The streets of Hangzhou throbbed with a daily pageant of tightrope walkers, strongmen, jugglers, acrobats, and animal trainers like the one above, whose monkey swings from a perch.

in the town, along with cat food and cat nests. These were decorative pets; for practical jobs like rat hunting, people kept long-haired working cats.

The well-to-do prided themselves on their landscaped gardens—enchanting worlds in miniature, containing artificial hills, curiously shaped stones, twisted trees, winding streams, and stands of bamboo. Walls pierced with windows were placed here and there to frame pretty views and lead the eye onward. Here, instead of swarms of poor in their dusty hemp jackets, trousers, and turbans, strolled ladies and gentlemen carrying parasols and wearing caps of black silk and long-sleeved silken robes of turquoise, vermilion, and purple, belted and buckled with jade, gold, and rhinoceros horn.

Theoretically, these costumes were regulated by sumptuary laws, legislation restricting the finest types of clothing (as well as the best furniture and housing) to those of high rank. In fact, such laws were ineffective. Imperial fashions were

freely imitated by the up-and-coming merchants, of which Hangzhou had many. These social climbers aped the court in every way, until, as one official put it, "In nine cases out of ten, if one looks a person over from head to foot, one will find that he is breaking the law."

Fortunately for at least some of the poor, it took a small army of servants to maintain the wealthiest households in style. Indeed, large retinues were a sign of success. Even prosperous courtesans had them. Much like the imperial staff with its various bureaus and departments, the corps of servants on a lavish estate was sub-divided into services that dealt with such distinct matters as fur-niture, alcohol and tea, table decoration and ceremonies for ban-quets, and kitchen duties. Great families had their own embroiderers and jewelers. And they supported private scholars, tutors, and

with the New Year, followed soon after by the Feast of Lanterns. Later came the Feasts of the New Fire, of the Dead, of Mid-Autumn, of Chrysanthemums, and of the Winter Solstice.

All of these were three-day festivals, and there were shorter holidays in between, affording the entire city ample opportuni-ty for revelry that often lasted through the night. The poor took to the streets, and those who could afford it headed to the pleas-ure boats of West Lake. The rich celebrated in their private gar-dens, which were so much a feature of the city that printed guides to Hangzhou had whole sections listing and describing them.

Among the most admired of the gardens were those at an estate in the hills north of Hangzhou belonging to the scholar-official Zhang Zu. Born in 1153, he was the grandson of the favorite general of Gaozong, first emperor of the Southern Song. Although

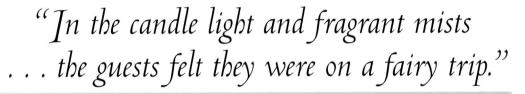

## "In the candle light and fragrant mists . . . the guests felt they were on a fairy trip."

poets, along with a host of entertainers—including people who trained performing insects.

These elaborate household staffs freed the upper classes to devote themselves to a busy annual round of festivities. The Chi-nese calendar was lunisolar, with the months determined by moons and the seasons by solstices and equinoxes. (Each month consisted of 29 or 30 days, with an extra month added to the 12-month year periodically to bring the lunar cycle back in harmo-ny with the solar cycle.) There were countless celebrations to mark the turning points of the year and the seasons, as well as the great days of the official Confucian cult of which the em-peror was head, the holy days of the Buddhists and Daoists, and the feast days of various deities. The seasonal festivities began

he served three times at court, Zhang Zu preferred to live in retirement, giving himself the curiously inappropriate name of "Master of the Frugality Studio."

Cultivated retirement was a Chinese tradition—Su Shi had turned his exiles into periods of meditation, scholarship, and study. But Zhang Zu's retreat, the expression of what he called "my small desire for peace and tranquillity," was far from being a quiet little place in the country. It had scores of pavilions, halls, and bridges, each with a name and special function such as watching the moon, reading books, or viewing the scenery, and all charmingly nestled among woods, streams, and ponds.

Perhaps the most delightful of these structures was Zhang's Riding-the-Mist pavilion, supported at a lofty height by iron

Inside the imperial gardens at Hangzhou, two children play beneath the delicate blossoms of a plum tree. Flowers were cherished by all of the southern capital's residents, including the emperor and his family. Hundreds of urns, containing exotic species of aromatic flowering plants and shrubs, surrounded the Palace of Coolness, one of many buildings in the imperial enclosure.

cables strung between pine trees. "On nights when the wind and moon were pure, together with guests he would ascend the pavilion with a ladder," wrote an admiring guest. Swaying there above the mists, the guest added, gave one the magical feeling of being borne aloft by "a flying immortal."

Even more elaborate than this were Zhang's many entertainments, such as the peony banquet. Ten times during the banquet, clouds of fragrance ushered in singing girls and courtesans bearing food and wine, with the girls costumed differently each time. "If they pinned white blossoms in their hair, they wore purple garments," a guest recalled. Later, purple blossoms were paired with pale yellow garments, and yellow blossoms with red garments. For each round they sang songs about peonies, and at the end of the banquet, they stood a hundred strong in rows to see the guests off. "In the candle light and fragrant mists, with singing and music all at once, the guests felt they were on a fairy trip," one enchanted visitor remarked.

Zhang's life was a carefully planned round of such elegant pleasures. As he told a friend, "Although my days of public service are many, I will not let them surpass in number my days of leisure." This, he believed, was philosophical perfection. His banqueting schedule for the year 1202, for instance, was called "The Coming Together of the Four Things," which were, according to a fifth-century poet, "good moments, attractive scenery, things that gratify the heart, and pleasurable events." In his preface to the schedule, Zhang vowed to pursue those four delights tastefully and generously, in keeping with Buddhist dharma, or teaching: "To do this with sincerity, not causing expense, labor, reckless misuse of objects, or carousal, is to have gratitude and reverence for what heaven has given us. A wise man of the past once said, 'Only when one can remain unstained by vulgar feelings is he able to expound the dharma and save other people.' "

The pursuit of such refined pleasures was not the way in which Su Shi had tried to save other people, but the world had

changed since Su's time. The heroic early years of the Southern Song were long gone, at least at court. Although there was always a faction longing to retake the conquered north and free the Chinese there from the yoke of the barbarians, the appeasement party prevailed. After fitful border clashes in 1161, 1165, and 1206, the Song continued to seek peace by paying tribute to the rulers of the north. Few people in fashionable Hangzhou worried about the distant frontiers, with their grim fortresses and gaunt troops. Nor were most officials much concerned with a threat that lay closer to home—the grueling poverty that left many in the cities, salt mines, and rice paddies little better off than those in the conquered north and largely indifferent to the fate of their empire.

One dedicated group of Chinese scholars known as the Neo-Confucianists, headed by the great philosopher Zhu Xi, scorned frivolity and self-indulgence and sought to revive the spirit of Confucius and his rigorous pursuit of wisdom and virtue. Although revered by later generations, these earnest scholars were resented by their contemporaries at court, who were in no mood for moralizing. The intrigue at the palace—which now had less to do with reform or other serious matters than with raw ambition—grew increasingly vicious over the years, and those who lost out sometimes paid with their lives.

Meanwhile, the spread of education, combined with corruption and cheating in the examination system, produced more successful scholars than the government could employ. Some chose not to sit for the examinations at all, preferring to become pet

**Pleasure boats gently glide by the magnificent homes that dot the shoreline of Hangzhou's West Lake in this 14th-century painting. The famous site probably appears much as it did two centuries earlier, when a patron at a nearby inn wrote, "Hill beyond green hill, pavilion behind pavilion—at the West Lake, will the singing and the dancing never cease?"**

scholars or poets to wealthy patrons like Zhang Zu and devote themselves to the good life. Even leading military men, who were looked down upon socially, tried to emulate the lavish civilian lifestyle. Many in government were less eager for high office than for a chance to retire to a world of pleasant surroundings and elegant entertainments. Everyone longed for a safe and gracious retreat. But few would find shelter from the fierce storm that was soon to descend on China from the north.

To those in and around the court at Hangzhou, the rising of the Mongol tribes on the steppes of central Asia at first seemed less of a threat than an opportunity. United under Chinggis, or Genghis, Khan, the conqueror who called himself "the flail of God," this latest and greatest wave of northern marauders swept down in the early 13th century and chal-

The south would not be easily taken, however. Threaded with water and quilted with rice paddies, it was no place for the cavalry attacks the Mongols favored, and its borders and cities were defended by stout fortifications and well-armed troops. The Mongols, however, were persistent and adaptable. Over the next four decades, they tightened their grip on the north and amassed the forces and equipment they would require to lay siege to the south. All the while, civilized life in Hangzhou went on much as it had before, seemingly oblivious to the threat. Although one impetuous official by the name of Jia Sidao would attempt to take forceful action in order to meet the Mongol threat, his efforts would misfire, and his name would be forever reviled.

Born in 1213, Jia was the son of a military family of some distinction but without great influence at court. He passed the government examination—by fraud, his enemies

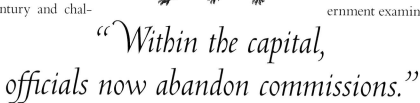

## "Within the capital, officials now abandon commissions."

lenged the Jin dynasty—as the Jurchens who ruled northern China and exacted tribute from the Song were known. In 1215 the Mongols succeeded in capturing the Jin capital of Zhongdu, at what is now Beijing. Ever merciless toward those who resisted them, they razed all the buildings to the ground and slaughtered the inhabitants.

In 1232, forgetting the lessons of their own history, the Song formed an ill-considered alliance with the Mongols to bring about the final collapse of the Jin. By 1234, Song forces had entered the old capital of Kaifeng, but only temporarily. The real victors were the Mongols, who now claimed northern China as their own and cast their hungry gaze on the rich lands and cities of their allies and soon-to-be enemies to the south.

claimed—while enjoying the frivolities of Hangzhou to the fullest, like many another of his generation. In fact, he would develop a reputation as a libertine, whose drinking, gambling, and sexual exploits would be seen as extreme even in Hangzhou.

When Jia was about 18, his elder sister became a concubine of the emperor Lizong, who fell deeply in love with her. Lizong could not make her empress, having recently married an unattractive but shrewd young woman named Xie Qiao, but he left no doubt that the lovely concubine had his heart when he raised her to the exalted rank of "Precious Consort." Her brother, for his part, would rise swiftly in the government ranks, and his detractors would charge that he owed his advancement chiefly to his sister's beauty.

Celebrating the New Year, a group of well-to-do women wrapped in sumptuous robes enjoy heaping plates of food and hot cups of tea *(top)* while being entertained by younger women playing percussion instruments and a horn. In the foreground, children commemorate the festival day in their own way—by setting off firecrackers, filled with an explosive compound that Europeans later adopted as gunpowder.

Yet Jia had his own talents, and he did well for himself both in office and in private ventures over the next few decades. He made a fortune and acquired many handsome properties in Hangzhou, some of which were grand indeed. One of them, Partial Repose, a reception hall in the hills above West Lake, could hold thousands of guests. Jia was something of a scholar as well, and he collaborated with a brilliant friend named Liao Yingzhong on a number of literary works, including a critical edition of Su Shi's poems.

In 1259, at the relatively young age of 46, Jia Sidao became Lizong's chief councilor. Some of his decisions in that capacity were good ones, as even his critics admitted. He brought the huge imperial clan, which tended to be greedy and faction-ridden, under control and even achieved a decree forbidding members of the royal family to hold executive office. And he eliminated eunuchs from influential positions at court, a recurring problem among the Song.

Those undertakings were minor, however, compared with his efforts to bolster the empire's defenses against the Mongols, who by the time he took office were growing increasingly belligerent. Ever since completing their conquest of the north, they had demanded tribute from the Song, who had staunchly refused, providing an excuse for Mongol incursions into Song territory. Jia set out to raise taxes—not to pay off the Mongols but to strengthen the imperial army and repel the enemy thrusts. Unfortunately, his proposals served to divide the Song leadership just when unity was most needed.

The Song were in dire financial straits, in part because of the enormous tracts of profitable farmland that were exempt from taxation. Among the privileged owners of those tracts were wealthy government officials, who opposed any attempts at land reform. But Jia managed to push through a measure that returned a third of private land over a set quota to the government, with the revenues going directly to the army. Despite outrage at the

court, Lizong stood firm, supporting his minister, and the measure remained in place. At the same time, Jia instituted an audit to prevent army officers—who already were resentful of civil authorities—from using allocated military funds for private transactions. The result of these actions was alienation at high levels and the defection of prominent officers and officials to the Mongol side. Jia was pilloried by his opponents, but he seemed indifferent to the attacks.

Lizong died in 1264 and was succeeded by Duzong, a brain-damaged, rather passive man who kept Jia Sidao as his chief

Nestled amid mountains, trees, and water, a country retreat offers arriving visitors the tranquillity of its beautiful pavilions and grounds, designed to put them at one with nature. In the garden, exotic animals wander undisturbed and a terrace overlooks a lake blooming with water lilies.

councilor and deferred to him. Meanwhile, Chinggis Khan's grandson, Khubilai Khan, had seized control of the Mongol Empire and was methodically preparing for the conquest of southern China. In 1268 Khubilai's forces paved the way for that assault by laying siege to two walled cities along the Song frontier, north of the Yangzi River. Those strongholds held out for more than four years, until one of them was overrun and its occupants slaughtered and the other was forced to surrender in order to avoid the same fate. The victorious Mongols then pressed southward to the Yangzi River and prepared themselves for a full-scale invasion of the south.

The Song empire was in disarray. Its military establishment was more contemptuous than ever of civilian rule—particularly the rule of Jia—and was riddled with defectors. The same could be said for the civilian ruling class in the provinces and at court: Few trusted in the strength of the empire, and fewer still in Jia. In desperation, he led forces into battle against the Mongols and suffered a disastrous defeat, giving his many enemies the long-awaited chance to oust him from power and send him into exile. Reportedly, the porters who carried him away in a sedan chair serenaded him with rude songs about his failings. Soon after, the exiled Jia was murdered.

It seemed as if the mandate of heaven had been withdrawn from the Song. Duzong died in 1274, to be succeeded by his four-year-old son. Empress Dowager Xie Qiao, Lizong's widow, served as the boy's regent. She was a formidable woman, but she faced an immense task in rallying her demoralized subjects, many of whose leaders were giving up without a fight. "Within the capital, officials now abandon commissions," she complained in a proclamation, "away from the capital, custodians relinquish seals and desert cities." Even imperial censors were forsaking their duties, she lamented, and fleeing in the night.

In December of 1274, with the Mongols poised to cross the Yangzi, the empress dowager issued an urgent appeal for volunteers to defend the beleaguered empire. The cause seemed hopeless, yet hundreds of thousands of loyalists would answer that call and make a desperate stand against the invaders.

# China's Littlest Subjects

The blessing "May you have many sons and a long life," bestowed upon a young Chinese woman by her mother-in-law, demonstrated not only the importance given to bearing and raising children in traditional Chinese society but also the value placed on having male children. Boys were especially hoped for in any family, since they could carry on the family's name, conduct ancestor worship, and if the family was of high standing, maintain their status and their hold on government positions. Although girls could help improve a family's lot by making a good marriage, they were generally viewed as something of a drain on the family's resources because they needed dowries to marry. And once married, a girl transferred her allegiance from her own family to that of her husband.

During China's Song dynasty, the size of one's family generally depended on economic status; among the wealthy, large numbers of children were desirable. But as the 11th-century scholar-poet Su Shi noted, poor farmers usually could raise only three children. To have more sons would mean dividing the family land into smaller parcels for inheritance, and more girls would mean more expenses for dowries. If more children were born to a family than could be cared for, they were likely to be placed with relatives, sent to monasteries, abandoned, or in some cases, sold as laborers or even drowned at birth.

This porcelain headrest from the Song dynasty depicts a young child resting contentedly on his belly. The Chinese favored hard pillows, and this one may have been used by women who were pregnant or who wanted to conceive.

Three youngsters seem mesmerized by goldfish swimming in bottles while an older child carries a younger one and a masked playmate tries to win the others' attention with his antics. Such paintings of children were very popular among the wealthy during the Song dynasty.

While older children clamor around their nurse, who is suckling a wriggling baby, a bare-bottomed child tries to climb into a peddler's basket. The peddler sells services as well as goods—a sign in the other basket reads "Skilled at doctoring cows, horses, and children."

# BRINGING CHILDREN INTO THE WORLD

An impending birth brought great excitement to a household. Before the delivery the mother's parents would send presents thought to hasten labor, including silver plates laden with flowers, baby clothes, and nuts and fruits such as chestnuts and jujubes. On the day of the birth and over the three weeks following, friends and relatives sent the mother useful gifts of rice, vinegar, and pieces of coal.

Parents paid great attention to the exact date and time of birth and recorded it for future consultations with astrologers on such matters as arranging trips, business deals, and marriages. On the child's first birthday, various objects were placed within reach, and prognostications about the baby's future vocation were made based on which object the child grasped.

Doctors commonly believed that breast-feeding threatened the mother's health, so many educated parents hired wet nurses. If the family could afford it, these women often stayed on to look after the children.

*"Not for one moment were they out of her mind; not a sliver of a step did she fail to take for them."*

Women of the court bathe and dress the emperor's children in this 12th-century painting. The wives and concubines of the emperor sometimes took care of their own children to ensure their safety.

Reenacting a Buddhist ceremony, children bathe a statue of Buddha. Children learned religious rituals by example and reinforced them through play.

> *"If they are taught the niceties, when grown they will not cause trouble through willful and arrogant behavior."*

A dutiful son, following Confucian teaching, kneels before his parents with an offering of food. His wife stands behind him with her own offering as their daughters look on.

## RAISING A RESPECTFUL CHILD

For most children, training in religious rituals and ancestor worship was informal and conducted within the family. It was generally limited to learning respect for older people and how to honor the ancestral cult, but sometimes the instruction included memorizing a few fragments of Buddhist text. Children usually were tutored by their mothers or grandmothers, and occasionally families invited monks or nuns into their homes to provide additional instruction.

Children of all classes were schooled in the Confucian concept of *xiao,* or respect for their elders. They learned the rituals of filial piety and the accepted rules of behavior, which included bowing before their elders, remaining standing until elders were seated, and accepting a drink when offered one by a superior. This doctrine, which permeated Chinese society, was not limited to one's own family—it also included respect for the emperor as the father of his people.

While the training of young girls included aspects of filial piety, they were taught mainly to be feminine, which meant being modest, respectful, reserved, and pleasant. A girl was not trained as extensively as her brother in ancestor rituals because once married, she became part of her husband's lineage; from then on, her primary obligation was to her husband and his parents.

# EDUCATION AND OCCUPATION

A child's education usually began with a mother teaching her sons and daughters to read and recite poems. Around the age of six, however, boys entered the world of their fathers and went to school or work. Girls were increasingly restricted to the women's quarters, where they were taught household duties.

Although some wealthy parents hired private tutors for their sons, most boys attended informal neighborhood schools. Usually held in a small rented room, the classes were often taught by candidates for civil service examinations. Peasant children occasionally attended these schools—their tuition paid by wealthy relatives—but more frequently they went straight to work as apprentices or farm hands.

When children reached adolescence, their schooling was generally finished. While some well-to-do students went on to government-sponsored higher learning, others found a mentor or followed their fathers into business or official positions.

With his friends gathered around him, a young scribe prepares to show off his brushwork in this 12th-century painting. Boys were taught calligraphy as part of the basic curriculum in local schools.

*"Mother was benevolent,*

*forgiving, and generous. . . .*

*She loved us to the utmost but never*

*let up in educating us."*

A little girl ducks beneath a length of newly woven silk cloth being ironed by older family members in this 12th-century scroll. Young girls began to learn household skills by shadowing their mothers as they did their chores.

97

# CHAPTER THREE

# The Mongol Conquest

As his mount gallops forward, a Mongol horseman twists back to fire his bow, a feat of agility perfected on the steppes of his homeland. Hardened by a harsh nomadic life on the plains, Mongols scorned China's city dwellers and farmers as sedentary weaklings, while the Chinese viewed the invaders as barbarians.

After a dazzling start, Wen Tianxiang had been something of a disappointment. In 1256, at the age of 20, he had placed first in the rigorous civil service examination in Hangzhou, earning rich praise from the emperor, who called him a heavenly portent—a play on the name "Tian," or "heaven." But then Wen's star faded. No sooner had he received his degree than his father died, and he dutifully withdrew into mourning. Afterward, he served for more than a decade without distinction in a series of provincial posts. Dismayed by his lack of progress, he retired from office in his mid-30s. A man of wealth and leisure with a wife and children and at least two concubines, he spent much of his time in the company of other scholars, reciting poetry, discussing literature, and carousing with singing girls.

All that changed, however, in December of 1274, when ominous rumblings to the north roused him from his lethargy. Mongol forces dispatched by Khubilai Khan, already firmly in control of northern China, were preparing to cross the Yangzi River and lay claim to the wealthy and fertile domain of the Southern Song. Empress Dowager Xie, acting on behalf of the boy emperor, her five-year-old grandson Gongdi, appealed to her countrymen to rise up and repel the invaders, and some 200,000 men answered the call. Wen was personally responsible for recruiting 10,000 troops in and around his home province of Jiangxi, in southeastern China.

That contribution to the war effort was much appreciated in Hangzhou, and Wen was summoned to the capital. Aside from composing stirring public pronouncements for the empress dowager, he took on a prominent role in the war ministry, a task to which he brought more enthusiasm than experience. Like other scholars, Wen hated the Mongols, whom he dismissed as "barbarian caitiffs," or base and despicable men. He swore to die rather than let his noble culture be "contaminated by barbarian blood." After years of frivolous mediocrity, he had found his calling.

· It would take more than zeal, however, to repulse the formidable Mongols. Notorious for their fast and furious campaigns on horseback, they adapted to circumstances and altered their tactics against the Southern Song, whose walled cities could be captured only through laborious siege warfare. Among the Mongol forces that crossed the Yangzi early in 1275 were legions of soldiers conscripted from northern China and other parts of the Mongol Empire, reinforced by hundreds of ships to counter the large Song navy and fearsome catapults designed by Muslim engineers to batter down Chinese fortifications.

In this as in earlier campaigns, the Mongols spared those in their path who surrendered promptly but massacred any who resisted, a fearful example to others inclined to put up a fight. In the autumn of 1275, after a siege of some six weeks that cost both sides staggering losses, the Mongols smashed through the walls of Changzhou, a vibrant city on the Grand Canal roughly 100 miles north of the Song capital. The victorious Mongol commander had warned the defenders that if they persisted in their "senseless and staunch resistance," not even their children would be spared, and he proceeded to

Defending a fortress, Song soldiers launch fragmentation bombs, which explode into deadly pieces. The Mongols also acquired such weapons, and they turned them against the Chinese.

In a 16th-century illustration of a 13th-century battle, Mongol troops storm across the Yangzi River on an ingenious bridge made of boats in order to lay siege to a city controlled by Song forces.

make good on his threat. Of the city's several hundred thousand inhabitants, only about 400 survived the ensuing massacre. Later, the conquerors piled up the corpses and covered them with dirt, leaving a mound up to 40 feet high and covering nearly an acre as a monument to their ferocity.

Such terror tactics paid off as the Mongols advanced toward the capital. Wen himself was now supervising the defenses of Pingjiang, another city on the Grand Canal, even closer to Hangzhou. But a few days after the massacre at Changzhou, he was recalled by his anxious superiors to the capital and took with him more than 30,000 of his best troops. Those left behind in Pingjiang yielded without a fight, and the defenders of other cities and towns followed suit, allowing the Mongols to advance virtually unopposed on Hangzhou.

In February 1276 Wen Tianxiang was sent to negotiate peace with the Mongols, but his manner toward them was so insolent that they took him captive. A short time later, the empress dowager, realizing that she was in no position to bargain, surrendered Hangzhou to spare the capital and its people from destruction and called upon Song loyalists everywhere to lay down their arms. She and the young emperor were taken into custody, and the Mongols occupied the capital in orderly fashion. After more than 300 years in power, the Song had seemingly given up the fight.

But the Mongols still had to reckon with die-hards such as Wen, who managed to escape a few weeks later from a train of imperial captives as they were being herded northward to the court of Khubilai Khan. Wen sought refuge with other defiant loyalists who had fled Hangzhou on the eve of its surrender and hurried south, where they rallied around the captured emperor's seven-year-old half brother, Shi. That fugitive prince and his younger sibling, Bing, represented the last slender hopes of Song partisans to preserve their dynasty. In June of 1276, in the city of Fuzhou on China's southeast coast, they crowned Shi emperor, hoping to muster enough support in the region to hold off the advancing Mongols.

Accompanied by attendants, Khubilai Khan *(center)* participates in a hunt wearing a Mongol coat of white ermine over rich Chinese brocades. During his reign, Khubilai appropriated certain aspects of Chinese culture to help legitimize his rule, including the adoption of a Chinese name, Yuan, for his new dynasty and the construction of a Chinese-style capital in what is now Beijing.

By the time Wen caught up with those loyalists, they were in disarray and in no mood to welcome another strong-willed insurgent. They found Wen arrogant and overbearing, and he soon went his own way, moving inland to conduct independent operations against the Mongols in his home province of Jiangxi. There he recruited a large and motley force that included scholars and poets, peasants, and even bandits. He hoped that a few decisive victories might stem the enemy tide, but his militia scored only small gains, and the Mongols exacted a heavy toll in return.

Wen sacrificed all for the cause, losing his fortune and his loved ones, including his wife, mother, sons, and daughters, all of whom died, disappeared, or fell into Mongol hands. In one of the poems he wrote during these years of duress, he likened his daughters, who were captured and sent north, to "young swallows without nests, shivering in the autumn chill." Finally, in January 1279, after most of his followers had been rounded up, Wen himself was seized. He swallowed poison to avoid being taken alive, but he survived, a prize captive of the Mongols he abhorred.

By then, the Song loyalists he left behind in Fuzhou had fled the oncoming Mongols and sailed down the coast from port to port before taking refuge on a mountainous island called Yaishan, set in a shallow bay off the mainland. Young emperor Shi had died during that hard journey—of fright, it was said—and to keep the dynasty alive, the loyalists had then crowned his six-year-old brother, Bing, emperor. Now Bing and as many as 200,000 supporters, most of them men and all of them determined to resist the Mongols to the last, were ensconced on Yaishan, living aboard their anchored ships or in makeshift lodgings.

In late February of 1279, a month or so after Wen's capture, the loyalists spotted enemy ships approaching and adopted a dubious defense. Trusting in their ships—some 1,000 in all, most of them powered by treadle-operated paddle wheels—they maneuvered the vessels into line and chained the largest of them together to form a massive bulwark. Sailors covered the sides of their wooden ships with matted linings to protect them against catapulted stones and flaming arrows.

The Song commanders knew that their fleet outnumbered the approaching enemy by about two to one, and they assumed that the attackers—whose ranks included Chinese conscripts and defectors—would attack immediately and risk all in a frontal assault. Instead, the Mongol forces bided their time and encircled the loyalist line, cutting the sailors off from supplies of fresh water. Many of them grew so desperate that they drank salt water and became sick.

The captive Wen Tianxiang was present at this confrontation, having been forced aboard a Mongol ship commanded by a Song defector, who now ordered him to urge his fellow loyalists to surrender. At the risk of execution, Wen refused, summing up his thoughts later in verse, "In this life since antiquity who can escape death, / Better to preserve a pure heart to illuminate the pages of history."

The commander spared Wen, however, and he lived to witness the last stand of the loyalists. At dawn on March 19, 1279, after harassing the Song for three weeks, the attackers closed in for the kill. Rain, clouds, and fog shrouded the area ominously, Wen wrote afterward, and the result seemed foreordained: "Heaven had already begun to mourn the certain losers."

The loyalists had hoped that the bay's shallow and shifting waters would keep their foes away, but Mongol ships exploited the outgoing tide that morning to launch a surprise attack from the direction of the mainland, and later in the day another squadron of warships rode the incoming tide and assailed the Song from the opposite direction. The Mongols had amassed the latest in Chinese weaponry, and their forces matched the loyalists blow for blow by unleashing rockets fueled by gunpowder as well as flaming arrows and catapult-launched bombs. It was among the fiercest fighting seen during the entire war. Wen watched with horror as

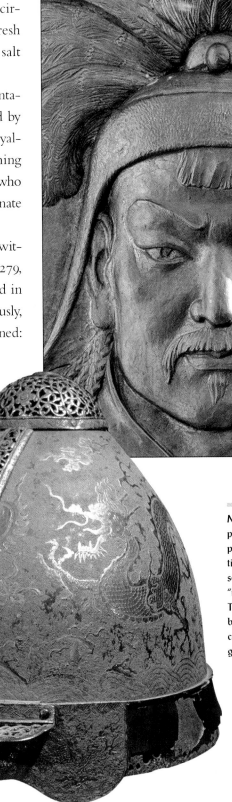

Mongol leader Chinggis Khan, portrayed above in a modern plaque, inspired terror in his victims and ambition in his successors, who, wrote a contemporary, "imitate his wicked cunning." The silver-inlaid helmet at left belonged to a high-ranking officer who served under Chinggis's grandson Khubilai Khan.

arrows descended like falling stars, leaving corpses "scattered like fibers of hemp" across the bloody surface of the bay.

At length one Song warship lowered its flag in surrender, and others followed. A few of the lighter and faster vessels managed to escape, but the larger ships were trapped. Many of those aboard refused to be taken prisoner by the dreaded Mongols and committed suicide by drowning. Caught in the middle of the doomed loyalist line was the emperor's own ship. To rally the troops, Bing's guardians had committed themselves and their emperor to this desperate battle. Now they too faced bondage or death.

The emperor's chief councilor did not hesitate to do what he saw as his duty. He compelled his wife and children to jump overboard to their deaths. Then he wrapped his arms tightly around Bing and

their subjects. Some Chinese qualified to serve as officials under the new regime would spurn the Mongols and retreat into obscure retirement. Others, like the captive Wen Tianxiang, would forfeit their lives rather than traffic with the invaders.

For several years after the battle at Yaishan, the Mongols refrained from executing Wen and tried to win him over. Khubilai Khan himself, a shrewd man who understood that China would be even harder to govern than to subdue, tried in vain to persuade Wen to accept high office, as one of his brothers had. "Same father, same mother," the prisoner wrote wistfully of his brother, "but not the same Heaven," a reference to the sacred place that was part of his own name and part of China's imperial mystique. Wen would never bow to Khubilai as the Son of Heaven. Finally in

## "Same father, same mother, but not the same Heaven."

leaped with him into the bay. The last Song emperor, clad in a royal yellow gown and weighed down by the imperial seals of gold that were strapped to his waist, sank beneath the surface of the water in his guardian's embrace. About half of the 200,000 loyalists perished with them that day—many by suicide—and the rest were taken prisoner.

For the Mongols the triumph at Yaishan capped the greatest of their military achievements. Since embarking on their far-ranging campaigns of conquest some 70 years earlier, they had laid claim to many lands—but none as populous and productive as China. Yet they never truly made this magnificent land their own. Officially, the victorious Khubilai Khan became the first emperor of a new Chinese dynasty. In reality, however, he and his Mongol successors would remain alien overlords, at odds with

1283, having spurned the enemy and preserved a "pure heart," he met with death at the hands of his captors, evincing to the last the proud spirit of defiance that would haunt the new masters of China for decades to come.

Although Khubilai Khan spent most of his life in China, his character was formed far to the north, in his rugged Mongolian homeland. It was there, in harsh conditions demanding courage and cunning, that the first great Mongol conqueror had emerged two generations earlier—Khubilai's notorious grandfather, Chinggis Khan, the man who initiated the conquest of China.

Legend had it that Chinggis was destined for violent exploits from birth, having emerged from his mother's womb grasping in his right hand "a clot of blood the size of a knucklebone." But

# ROCKET ARROWS AND COSMIC ENGINES

Inventions flourished in China during the Song and Yuan dynasties, when engineers boosted trade by building locks on canals to safely raise and lower boats, textile workers revolutionized the silk industry with the spinning wheel, and military commanders defended the ramparts of their cities with flame throwers and bombs. This flurry of activity was part of a centuries-long tradition of Chinese innovation.

The inventions often had come about in surprising ways. Alchemists, seeking an elixir of immortality and a way of converting base metals into gold, created the explosive substance that would be known as gunpowder. The magnetic compass was developed by Chinese geomancers, specialists hired to calculate the proper placement of structures such as houses and tombs so they would be harmoniously aligned with the earth's forces—which required precise directional knowledge. Working for the throne, astronomers devised complex observational instruments and kept records of eclipses and comets to bolster the authority of the emperor, who had to explain any unusual celestial phenomena in keeping with his mandate from heaven.

These inventions and many others originated in China or were adopted by the Chinese centuries before they appeared in Europe. While ancient Greek and Roman horses struggled to pull loads harnessed to them by choking neck straps, the Chinese oxen easily moved heavy loads with a padded collar harness strapped across the sternum. By the Song and Yuan eras, the Chinese were printing books using movable type and woodblock printing, while Western scribes still laboriously hand copied manuscripts one by one. The chain drive, the crank handle, the wheelbarrow, and the umbrella all appeared in China first. A few of the more noteworthy inventions either created or adopted early on by the Chinese are listed in the timeline below, and some from the Song and Yuan dynasties are described on the following pages.

| 400-200 BC | 200-1 BC | AD 1-200 | AD 200-400 | AD 400-600 | AD 600-800 |
|---|---|---|---|---|---|
| magnetic compass | paper | suspension bridge | fishing reel | paddle-wheel boat | brandy and whiskey |
| kite | miniature hot-air balloon | rudder | stirrup | essentials of | block printing |
| crossbow | wheelbarrow | seismograph | porcelain | steam engine | |
| | | | umbrella | | |
| | | | matches | | |
| | | | helicopter rotor and | | |
| | | | propeller | | |

A 14th-century Chinese foot soldier aims his portable rocket launcher, which will send a barrage of rocket arrows soaring through the air. China's soldiers could fire tens of thousands of rockets in a single battle.

| AD 800-1000 | AD 1000-1200 | AD 1200-1400 |
|---|---|---|
| paper money | movable-type printing | metal-cased bombs |
| gunpowder | spinning wheel | land mines |
| chain drive | rocket | sea mines |
| smallpox inoculation | | multistage rockets |
| flamethrower | | |
| fireworks | | |
| canal pound lock | | |

## LAUNCHING ROCKET ARROWS

Around 1150 the Chinese discovered that one could shoot arrows without a bow by attaching gunpowder to an arrow's shaft and then igniting it. A gunpowder charge was wrapped in oiled paper and strapped to the shaft near the arrowhead *(left)*, and an iron weight was fixed at the rear for balance. With the counterweight, the arrow could fly some 500 to 1,100 feet without nosediving.

The Chinese built wood or bamboo rocket launchers, like the modern reproduction at left, to hold batches of rocket arrows and help aim them. The launchers' conical shape helped disperse the arrows over a wide area. Arms makers devised various types of launchers with descriptive names like "Five-tigers-springing-from-a-cave-rocket-arrows" and "Mr.-Facing-Both-Ways-rocket-arrow-firing-basket."

Such rocket arrows proved extremely effective in warfare, especially when a barrage was fired. Wheelbarrows, an earlier Chinese invention, transported batteries of rocket launchers on the battlefield so that as many as 320 rockets could be launched at once. Arrows were made even deadlier by the practice of coating them with poison.

The Song devised bombs as well as rockets, encasing the early models in bamboo or porcelain and later ones in metal. One 11th-century military leader observed that enemy forces hit with these explosives "fled, howling with fright."

A printer gently rubs a pad over the paper placed on the inked type *(left)*, a folded stack of blank sheets on the table beside him. Below, a compositor sits between Wang Chen's revolving tables, which held some 60,000 characters in special compartments. One table stored commonly used characters, while the other held rarely used ones.

## PRINTING WITH MOVABLE TYPE

Between 1041 and 1048, a Song commoner named Bi Sheng made the world's first movable type. According to a description written a few decades later, he "took sticky clay and cut in it characters as thin as the edge of a coin," and fired the pieces to harden them. He then placed a metal frame on an iron plate coated with a mixture of paper ashes, pine resin, and wax to help hold the type, and set the characters in place. Ink was brushed onto the type and a sheet of paper placed over it and rubbed with a pad. The paper was then peeled off and dried. The Song also began printing on pages sewn into a volume rather than pasted together to form a continuous scroll.

Since written Chinese comprises thousands of different characters, Bi Sheng stored his clay characters in marked wooden cases sorted not by individual characters but in groups of characters whose sounds rhymed. In the early 14th century an official named Wang Chen devised a more convenient storage and handling system, keeping the type —sometimes made of wood or bronze instead of clay—in large revolving tables *(right)*. But the vast number of characters in the Chinese language made movable type unwieldy except for printing several thousand copies of a publication. Block printing—where the text was carved onto blocks, then brushed with ink—remained the preferred method in Yuan China.

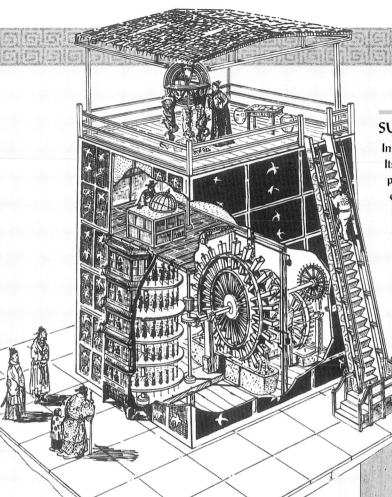

## SU SONG'S COSMIC ENGINE

In 1092 an official named Su Song built the first truly mechanical clock. Its purpose was not for ordinary people to tell time, however, but to provide data for casting royal horoscopes. In determining which of an emperor's offspring should succeed him, court astrologers looked for the best horoscope—based on the year, day, and hour of conception. As seen in the cutaway reconstruction at left, a huge waterwheel with scoops that filled every quarter-hour powered the gears of the 39-foot-high so-called Cosmic Engine. Wrote Su Song, "The heavens move without ceasing and so also does water flow and fall." Gears rotated five platforms of puppets, visible at the tower's front. The figures announced the quarter-hour by beating a drum and every two hours by ringing a bell. The clock's gears also turned an armillary sphere *(top)*, which was positioned under a movable roof and synchronized to follow the planets' motions. Su's invention operated from 1092 to 1126, when Kaifeng fell and it was dismantled and taken away.

Chinese astronomers compiled maps of up to 1,434 stars, including the 10th-century star map at right, which shows the Big Dipper *(bottom)* and its neighboring constellations. The imperial family was associated with various stars, the emperor most commonly with the polestar.

before he could cut a bloody swath through foreign lands, he first had to deal with local challengers. The Mongols subsisted by hunting and herding, moving frequently on horseback to fresh pastures, a roving existence that promoted conflict among the various tribes. Virtually every male between 14 and 60 years of age was ready and able to fight, and tribal chieftains vied for supremacy by amassing formidable fighting bands.

After many travails Chinggis emerged as the greatest of those chieftains, with devoted and disciplined troops and a superb cavalry. In 1206, when he was around 40, he succeed in uniting the diverse and contentious tribes of Mongolia. That year, at a grand assembly, his fellow Mongols recognized him as their supreme leader and conferred on him the name *gurkhan,* meaning "universal ruler." In accepting that title, he proudly hoisted aloft his white standard with its nine horsetails and declared that heaven had ordained him to "rule all nations."

Although he would not quite fulfill that sweeping mandate, the man known to posterity as Chinggis Khan would harness the combative energies of his people and drive them to astonishing feats. At the time there were probably no more than one and a half million people in all of Mongolia. But the rigors of a nomadic existence conditioned even the women and children to hardship and equipped them to travel with the fighting forces and support them in battle when necessary. And the men possessed special qualities as soldiers that were seldom found among farmers or city dwellers. At the age of three, a boy was taught to ride by his mother, who tied him onto the horse. He was given his first bow and arrows a year or so later. Life on the wind-whipped steppe, with its searing heat in summer and its arctic blasts in winter, hardened him to privation. He could go 10 days without cooking a meal, subsisting on dried milk curd, fermented mare's milk, and cured beef or mutton. If necessary, he would eat carrion or would open a vein in the shaggy neck of his mount and sip its blood.

Those horses were small of stature but unsurpassed for stamina, capable of covering more than 60 miles a day for days on end. Mongols on campaign might appear slovenly—the men were not given to bathing and sometimes reeked of alcohol—but they conformed to a stern military code that prescribed death for almost any breach of discipline. A soldier lived up to what Chinggis called "the great principle," unswerving loyalty, or paid with his life. Chinggis reinforced that loyalty by sharing in the men's

privations and urging his aides to do the same. "Only a man who feels hunger and thirst, and by this estimates the feelings of others," he told them, "is fit to be a commander."

Soon after uniting Mongolia in 1206, Chinggis led his forces on the first of many foreign campaigns. Those ventures may have been dictated in part by a climate that had turned colder and reduced the supply of grass for the herds in their homeland, impelling the Mongols to seek bounty through conquest. But they and their avid leader needed little prompting to go to war. They loved to fight and pillage, and the unification allowed them to do so on an unprecedented scale. "The greatest joy," Chinggis reported-

This copy of a Song-era hand scroll portrays life among a group of northern nomads, whose only homes are tents pitched in the stark landscape of their native land—a barbaric existence in the eyes of most Chinese.

ly told a comrade, "is to conquer one's enemies, to pursue them, to seize their belongings, to see their families in tears, to ride their horses, and to possess their daughters and wives."

Although Mongol forces would fan out in many directions in the decades to come, it was China, the wealthy colossus to their south, that they coveted first and last. Chinggis prepared for his assault on northern China by sweeping down around its western flank and subduing a Tibetan people called the Tanguts, whose abject king gave Chinggis one of his daughters as a peace offering in 1209—one of more than 500 wives the Great Khan reportedly took in his lifetime. The Tanguts also paid tribute with herds of magnificent white camels. The Mongols were now in a position to avoid China's northern frontier, fortified by earthen ramparts that served much the same defensive purpose as the Great Wall that was completed in later times.

Chinggis invaded China from the west with an army of little more than 100,000 men, whereas the opposing force consisted of more than 400,000 soldiers. But in this campaign as in later ones, the Mongols pressed into service men in the areas they conquered, so that their army swelled as it advanced. The most useful conscripts were those who felt little loyalty to the Mongols' foes, and there were many such men in and around northern China, whose border areas had always been hard for emperors to control and whose present rulers—the Jin, or Jurchens—were themselves intruders from the north. In their campaign against the Jin, the Mongols fought as cavalry and amassed their infantry from the local populace. Even in areas that were resolutely hostile to them, the Mongols man-

Wielding a grisly skeletal toy, Death lures an infant away from his sister as their nursing mother looks on with resignation. Death was a frequent visitor to Chinese families, particularly in the desperate years of the Mongol occupation, when the population of China plummeted.

Beggars remained an all-too-common sight in China through the ages, despite relief efforts by successive emperors, including Khubilai Khan.

aged to bolster their strength by forcing the rural population to march in front of their assault columns so that the defenders would be reluctant to use their weapons.

The Mongols met with increasing resistance as they left the frontier behind and swept east across the populous core of northern China toward the Jin capital of Zhongdu, at what is now Beijing. Few who opposed them were spared. In all, they reduced some 90 cities to rubble before sacking and devastating Zhongdu in 1215. The imperial palace went up in flames, but the Jin royal family escaped south to the old capital of Kaifeng, where they held out as the rulers of a much-reduced domain for nearly 20 years before the Mongols completed the conquest of northern China. These grim campaigns marked the beginning of a steep decline in China's population, from about 100 million at the dawn of the 13th century to between 60 million and 80 million in the 14th century, a decline attributable to the brutal Mongol conquests and to the famines and epidemics that followed.

The toll might have been even steeper had the Mongols treated the Chinese as they did some other peoples they subjugated. In 1225, for example, the Tanguts along China's western frontier turned rebellious, and Chinggis set out to destroy them, leaving their country a wasteland, littered with human bones. Fortunately, at least one adviser to Chinggis recognized that it would be the height of folly for the Mongols to lay waste to the defeated Chinese and use their bountiful land simply as pasture for their herds. During the conquest of northern China, Chinggis met with a wise man named Yelü Chucai, who had served as councilor to the Jin king and knew how to oblige conquerors. He was an astrologer and soothsayer, among other things, and Chinggis used him to forecast the success of military expeditions by examining the cracks in a sheep's shoulder blade—a time-honored divination procedure.

But Yelü was also a shrewd councilor. He reportedly advised Chinggis to leave the Chinese who had survived the conquest in possession of their lives and their land and to profit by their toil. "You should tax land and commerce," he urged, "and should make profits on wine, salt and iron, and the produce of mountains and marshes." The Mongol ruler took that advice and set a profitable precedent for his successors.

Chinggis died in 1227, and two years elapsed before the far-flung Mongol nobles and warlords could gather in council and confirm his son Ögödei as his successor. Ögödei completed the conquest of northern China in 1234 and farmed out the collection of taxes there to the highest bidders—who then imposed astronomical tax rates on the conquered populace, perhaps as high as 60 or 70 percent, with devastating effects on the economy.

Later Mongol rulers of China would have to reckon with the consequences of that ruinous policy. Ögödei himself was more concerned with expanding the Mongol domain, which already extended from the Pacific Ocean west to the Caspian Sea. During Ögödei's reign, Mongol forces swelled by Turks and Persians swept westward to Moscow and Kiev and south into the Middle East. They sacked cities in Poland and Hungary and were preparing to assault the walls of Vienna when the death of Ögödei late in 1241 halted their ferocious advance. Western Europe was spared devastation only because the Mongol leaders had to return to their homeland to elect a new Great Khan.

Since there were no strict rules of succession among the Mongols, the election process was often long and contentious. Women of the Mongol ruling family exerted great influence over the nobles and sometimes determined the outcome. Ögödei's widow managed to have his preferred successor passed over in favor of their son Güyüg. And after Güyüg died in 1248, another remarkable woman, Sorghaghtani Beki, herself from a noble Mongolian family, successfully pressed the claims of her sons by Tolui, a hard-fighting, hard-drinking son of Chinggis who had died around 1232, when his son Khubilai was in his late teens. At her urging, Khubilai's older brother Möngke was elected Great Khan in 1251, and Khubilai succeeded him in 1260, at the age of 45.

Although he was officially the ruler of the entire Mongol Empire, Khubilai's actual domain was limited to China and surrounding lands, including the Mongolian homeland, while lesser khans ruled more distant regions. His overriding ambition was to defeat the Southern Song—in part to prove himself to his Mongol followers, who were always hungry for glory and spoils. But more than that, he needed to conquer the south to forestall any attempt by the Song at regaining the northern regions they once ruled

This portrait of Marco Polo, Venetian merchant and famous chronicler, decorated the title page of an edition of *The Travels of Marco Polo* produced in Nuremberg in 1477. Dictated by Polo around 1300, the book includes descriptions of life in China during the reign of Khubilai Khan.

and to bring the wealthiest and most productive part of China within the scope of his avid tax collectors.

Compared with his grandfather Chinggis and his uncle Ögödei, Khubilai was an enlightened despot. Before becoming Great Khan, he had ruled part of northern China and had learned something of Chinese ways. One of his closest advisers was a Chinese scholar, a former Buddhist monk named Liu Bingzhong, whose multiple skills in calligraphy, painting, mathematics, and astronomy much impressed Khubilai. In a long memorial to the Great Khan on policy and administration, Liu reminded him of an old Chinese saying: "One can conquer the world on horseback; one cannot govern it on horseback."

Yet Khubilai remained very much a conqueror in the harsh Mongol tradition. In the campaign against the south, his generals operated much as their predecessors had against the north. If fewer cities were razed in the south, it was not because the Mongols moderated their tactics but because the Song were unwilling to bear the terrible cost of defying the invaders and surrendered most of their population centers without a fight. But the final victory over the Song at Yaishan in 1279 was just the beginning of a long struggle for Khubilai, inheritor of the bloody legacy of Chinggis, to achieve legitimacy in a land where rulers were honored more for benevolence than for brute force.

By the time he conquered the south, Khubilai Khan had already moved his court from Karakorum in Mongolia to a new capital in northern China, known to posterity as Beijing. Built near the ruins of the Jin capital destroyed by Chinggis in 1215, this lavish imperial seat was planned by Khubilai's Chinese adviser Liu Bingzhong. A force of up to 28,000 laborers, directed by a Muslim architect, began the mammoth project in 1266, and the first government buildings were ready for occupancy six years later. When completed, the walled capital covered 24 square miles, encompassing handsome avenues, spacious squares, and res-

idences interspersed with lakes, gardens, and bridges. This was a dramatic change of scene for a ruler whose people had roamed the steppes on horseback and slept in tents, but Khubilai was determined to live up to China's grand imperial traditions. Emulating the Chinese reverence for ancestors, he even had a temple in honor of his forebears erected near the palace grounds.

No one did more to bring this great capital—and the Great Khan himself—to the attention of the world than a Venetian chronicler named Marco Polo, who reportedly reached China around 1275 in the company of his father and uncle, veterans of an earlier journey to China, and remained there as Khubilai's guest for 17 years. Marco Polo's account of his travels, published after he returned to Italy, astonished Europeans, who could scarcely believe his tales of oriental splendor. Indeed, scholars would later question the veracity of his account and debate whether he ever made the journey described in his narrative. If he did not visit China himself, however, he certainly based his chronicle on the tales of those who had, for his portrait of Khubilai's realm, while not entirely credible, was consistent in many respects with other historical sources.

He related, for example, that the suburbs of Khubilai's new capital contained "quite twenty thousand prostitutes," who serviced merchants and other foreigners visiting the capital. That number was probably inflated, but Hangzhou and other Chinese cities of the day teemed with prostitutes, and the Mongol conquest might well have reduced even more women than usual to prostitution. Marco Polo added that they were required by way of taxation to offer their services free of charge to special foreign guests of the Great Khan.

All those in the vicinity of Khubilai had to remain "humble, quiet, and calm," he reported, and each baron or noble visiting the court carried "a vase small and beautiful" to use as a spittoon. "They have likewise certain beautiful slippers of white leather which they carry with them, and when they are arrived at the court if they wish to go into the hall, supposing that the lord asks for them, they put on these white slippers so as not to soil the beautiful and cunningly made carpets of silk."

Khubilai's palace, Marco Polo added, was "the greatest and most wonderful that ever was seen," with more than 400 chambers, one of them so great "that more than six thousand men would well feed there at once." Near the palace stood a man-made mound of earth 100 paces high with an ornamental pavilion on its summit and its sides covered by transplanted trees: "Whenever his majesty receives information of a handsome tree growing in any place, he causes it to be dug up, with all its roots and earth about them, and however large and heavy it may be, he has it transported by means of elephants to this mount, and adds it to the verdant collection." Such extravagance was in keeping with Chinese imperial traditions. The ill-fated emperor Huizong had done much the same when stocking his pleasure park in Kaifeng.

Khubilai had to balance his role as emperor of China with that of ruler of the Mongols. While adopting many Chinese customs and attempting to appease his conquered subjects, he also sought to preserve his ancestral identity and honor Mongol traditions. Screens of ermine skin stood in his sleeping chambers to remind him of the hunt. His sons and their cousins forsook the comfortable palace and lived in Mongol-style tents pitched on the imperial grounds amid grass he had transplanted from the steppes of the homeland. Many Mongols wore their traditional garb of furs and leather, although Khubilai himself usually presided at court robed in Chinese fashion. He forbade intermarriage between Mongols and Chinese and took only Mongol women as consorts—by the score, according to Marco Polo: "Every second year a hundred maidens, the most beautiful to be found in all that race, are chosen and are brought to the Great Khan as he may wish."

## CERAMICS OF CHINA

By the dawn of the Song dynasty, the shortage of copper had transformed the production of ceramics in China into a major industry. Artisans who had formerly crafted their wares from copper and bronze began to work with clay. Chinese potters created everything from fine art objects to everyday cups and bowls. Among the most famous ceramics are China's lustrous blue-and-white porcelains *(left)*; their production reached artistic heights during the Yuan dynasty.

To produce the distinctively colored porcelains, artisans painted a bright blue pigment, made out of cobalt oxide imported from the Near East, on partially dried clay objects. They then covered their work with a clear glaze and fired it. A wide range of pigment tones could be achieved with this process.

Khubilai encouraged the production and export of ceramics, which were second only to silk in value as an export. To appeal to Mongol taste, Yuan potters often used more elaborate ornamentation than their Song predecessors, some of it inspired by Near Eastern metalwork and by popular Chinese drama. The 14th-century wine jar at left is decorated with scenes from a romantic play entitled *The West Chamber*.

His Mongol heritage was most evident at his summer capital of Shangdu, some 160 miles north of Beijing, where Khubilai and his court retreated annually to avoid the stifling heat. Every August at Shangdu, to ensure a year of good luck, the Great Khan performed the Mongol ritual of scattering mare's milk while bowing to heaven and calling out the name of his revered grandfather, Chinggis. In the midst of Khubilai's spacious game reserve at Shangdu stood a large palace with a roof crafted of gilded and varnished cane and covered with paintings of beasts and birds—the inspiration for the "stately pleasure dome" evoked centuries later as Xanadu, Samuel Taylor Coleridge's poem "Kubla Khan," based on Marco Polo's account of the place he called Ciandu, or Shangdu.

From this summer palace Khubilai pursued the old Mongol pastime of hunting. A huge retinue of falconers, hunters, and soldiers accompanied him on his expeditions. Sometimes, they took along trained lions, leopards, and lynxes to chase down the stags, bears, and other quarry that roamed the park. Marco Polo claimed that when he first met Khubilai, the emperor was neither too fat nor too lean but "well formed in all parts." In later years, however, too much drinking and feasting on mutton and other fatty meats transformed the athletic horseman into a portly spectator, who observed the hunt from a palanquin, or litter, so large that it took several elephants to support it. "He always goes on four elephants," Polo recounted, "on which he has a very beautiful wooden room, which is all covered inside with cloth of beaten gold and outside it is wrapped round and covered with lion skins, in which room the great Khan always stays when he goes hawking because he is troubled with the gout."

Despite his fondness for hunting and feasting, Khubilai was far from being an idle or frivolous ruler. He was intent on proving to his subjects that he had not just the might but the right to rule China. Unlike earlier emperors, he could not name his dynasty after his homeland without calling attention to his alien origins, so he settled on the term Yuan, which possessed such weighty meanings as "origins of the universe" and "primal force" in Chinese literature.

His edict establishing the Yuan dynasty referred to it as embodying benevolence, and in fact this grandson of the fearsome Chinggis made calculated efforts to live up to the Confucian ideal of the merciful ruler—so long as he reaped rewards in the bargain. He favored the old Mongol practice of allowing certain groups of criminals to pay fines to avoid punishment, which helped to replenish the imperial treasury. And he reduced the number of executions carried out in China each year to a few dozen. "Prisoners are not a mere flock of sheep," he admonished his officials. "How can they be suddenly executed?" Then he added, "It is proper that they be instead enslaved and assigned to pan gold with a sieve."

Khubilai also recognized that peasants whose lives and lands had been devastated by the conquest would have to be granted some relief if they were ever to become dependable sources of revenue for the Mongols. The imperial court provided grain to widows and orphans, and taxes were occasionally waived in war-torn areas. In addition, he reinstituted some of the measures taken by earlier dynasties to guard against famine. New granaries were built—58 in Beijing alone—to store surpluses from plentiful harvests for distribution in times of want. Marco Polo reported that Khubilai sent out "trusty messengers and inspectors" regularly

of no fewer than 1,400 stations, stocked with some 50,000 horses as well as 6,700 mules and 8,400 oxen for carrying heavier loads and nearly 6,000 boats for plying the waterways. Urgent messages were carried by mounted men between stations 25 miles or so apart. Messengers obtained a fresh horse at each station and, under ideal conditions, covered 250 miles a day. According to Marco Polo, each station had a comfortable hostelry for the postmen and other wayfarers, replete with plush beds "furnished with rich silk cloths."

Such accomplishments did more to serve the interests of China's Mongol overlords, however, than to benefit their subjects. Although Khubilai adopted the trappings of past emperors, he never

## *"Prisoners are not a mere flock of sheep. How can they be suddenly executed?"*

to determine which provinces had been afflicted by drought, plague, or pestilence and had need of assistance in the form of tax relief or dole from his granaries.

Besides the construction of the new capital at Beijing, Khubilai undertook other mammoth public works projects, employing forced labor. Some three million workers extended the Grand Canal northward from the vicinity of the Yellow River for 135 miles so that it reached nearly to Beijing, thus linking Khubilai's capital with the rich cities and fertile fields to the south.

Perhaps the most ambitious of Khubilai's projects was a vast system of postal relay stations that linked the capital with the rest of the nation. The Mongols had long relied on relays of men on horseback to carry dispatches from one part of their domain to another. Khubilai hoped to gain tighter control over China by establishing a similar delivery system for official mail, consisting

acquired their most important asset—a dedicated corps of Chinese officials, equipped to serve as intermediaries between rulers and their subjects. Despite the presence at his court of men like Liu Bingzhong, he had no intention of entrusting the government of China largely to the Chinese. He refused to reinstitute the civil service examination and instead appointed his leading officials from among an exotic coterie that included central Asian Muslims, Turks, Russians, and Persians.

Those imported bureaucrats stood second in the Yuan hierarchy after the Mongols themselves, of whom there were no more than a few hundred thousand in China. The northern Chinese (who included a number of Jurchens and others from beyond China's traditional borders) ranked third, and the southerners—suspect because they had been only recently conquered—came last. All Chinese were subject to stricter punishments than non-

Chabi, Khubilai's influential senior wife, wears a *bakhtakh*, the traditional Mongol headdress of a married woman. Impressed by the glories of China's past, Chabi encouraged her husband to emulate the great emperors of earlier dynasties.

Chinese and were forbidden to congregate in public or own weapons; they were even prohibited from dealing in bamboo because it could be used for making bows and arrows.

As evidenced by his international corps of advisers and administrators, Khubilai was generally tolerant of foreigners and their beliefs so long as they served his interests. His mother belonged to the Nestorian Church, an offshoot of Christianity, and he looked favorably not only on Christians but on Buddhists, Muslims, and Jews. "I do honor and reverence to all four," he reportedly told Marco Polo in reference to those faiths. His professed respect for the major religions stemmed in part from a recognition of their possible political value. But he also harbored the superstitious hope that their various holy men might be able to imbue his dynasty with magic and power.

Khubilai's wife Chabi was an ardent Buddhist and helped to indoctrinate him in that faith. Chabi wielded the most clout of his four principal wives, each of whom presided over a separate household that included subordinate wives and concubines. She had a reputation for frugality, encouraging court ladies to collect strings from the army's discarded bows and make them into thread that could be woven into cloth. She was also something of a fashion designer, remodeling the traditional Mongol hat to include a brim to protect horsemen from the desert sun.

At first, Chabi and Khubilai flirted with the prevalent Chinese form of Buddhism—Chan (known as Zen in Japan)—which was concerned less with matters of doctrine than with the personal search for enlightenment. But it proved to be too abstract and unworldly for them, and they soon turned to Tibetan Buddhism, which had more exotic rituals and a tradition of political involvement on the part of its spiritual leaders. Khubilai and Chabi even gave their firstborn son a Tibetan name, Dorji.

Khubilai's guru was a leading Tibetan lama. The delicate

question of who was to take precedence—temporal ruler or spiritual leader—was resolved by a compromise proposed by Chabi. When Khubilai was receiving private religious instruction, he sat on a lower platform than the lama. But when conducting court business in public, he always occupied the higher platform. The lama introduced to the court pomp-filled rituals such as a procession known as Suppression of the Demons and Protection of the State. In return, Khubilai granted the lama jurisdiction over Tibet and contributed funds and land for building Tibetan Buddhist temples and monasteries.

Like other privileges extended to foreigners by Khubilai, the favoritism shown to Tibetan holy men alienated many Chinese. One Tibetan monk employed by the government was so zealous at promoting his faith in southern China that he not only con-

Khubilai Khan supervises the exchange of gold and silver for paper money in an illustration from a 14th-century edition of Marco Polo's book. Ninth-century Chinese traders began using paper as a solution to the problems of handling great numbers of coins and a shortage of copper; paper money became common under the Mongols.

verted former Song imperial halls around Hangzhou into temples and shrines but also financed his work by pillaging the tombs of Song royalty. His men extracted gold, silver, jade, and other treasure buried with the emperors and empresses and scattered their remains about, prompting a group of outraged Chinese scholars to gather up the royal bones and rebury them in secret.

No group of foreigners met with greater hostility in China, however, than the Muslims. Imported from Persia and central Asia—frequently by force—they served the Great Khan as military engineers, architects, physicians, astronomers, and court musicians and poets. Muslim merchants imported camels, horses, carpets, spices, and precious stones from abroad and exported textiles, ceramics, lacquer ware, ginger, and silks. But above all, Muslims served as Khubilai's tax collectors—and financial scapegoats, drawing the fury of overburdened Chinese subjects who might otherwise have blamed all their problems on the Mongols. Khubilai allowed the Muslims to claim a share of the proceeds, and they turned the balance over to the imperial treasury. While some hard-pressed Chinese received tax relief, most paid steep rates to finance Khubilai's lavish new imperial capital and the extension of the Grand Canal, among other works—and Muslims received much of the blame.

One of the most hated officials in China was a central Asian Muslim named Ahmad, who served as Khubilai's finance minister for 20 years. Whatever Ahmad's personal flaws—the Chinese accused him of nepotism and profiteering—his major sin was having to raise vast amounts of money for his Mongol masters. He not only hiked taxes but also borrowed a page from past dynasties by imposing state monopolies on the profitable trades in tea, liquor, and salt. A cabal of Chinese conspirators finally assassinated him, and Khubilai promptly had the assassins rounded up and executed. But when a crown jewel turned up in Ahmad's house—perhaps planted there by his Chinese foes—the Great Khan changed his tune. At his insistence, several of Ahmad's sons were put to death and his corpse was exhumed and publicly mutilated.

Nothing Khubilai did to shift the blame, however, could long disguise the fact that the Mongols were bleeding China dry. Overtaxation sapped the economy and left less for Khubilai's successors to exploit. To make matters worse, gold, silver, and other precious metals were flowing out of China as foreign tax collectors sent their earnings home. Khubilai tried to compensate for the shortage of cash by printing paper currency—notes that Marco Polo claimed were honored "as if they were of pure gold or silver." Over the decades, however, the Yuan dynasty printed more and more of this paper money to try to cover its financial shortcomings, causing runaway inflation.

Such problems, rooted in the policies of Khubilai's predecessors, might have been alleviated if he had been willing to abandon his role as world conqueror and devote himself to China. But for much of his reign, he was engaged in costly conflicts with rival Mongols and with Asians beyond China's borders whom he hoped to subjugate. Despite Khubilai's attempts to demonstrate that he had not lost his cultural identity, Mongol leaders within his own family interpreted his every concession to Chinese civilization as an affront to their traditions and contested his right to rule. After beating back an early challenge from his younger brother, Arigh Böke, Khubilai was opposed by a nephew, Khaidu, ruler of central Asia—a conflict that dragged on for years—and by his cousin, Nayan, whose rebellion in Manchuria was crushed. Nayan was executed in the manner traditional for Mongol nobles, by being dragged to death by horses while wrapped in a carpet so that not a drop of his noble blood would be spilled.

One way for Khubilai to reinforce his standing among the Mongols was to engage in fresh conquests, but he had little success beyond the bounds of China. Korea yielded to him early in his reign and paid him annual tribute that reportedly included special fish skins, used to make shoes for Khubilai's gout-swollen feet. But his campaigns into the jungles of Southeast Asia against Annam and Champa—in modern-day Vietnam—bogged down, and a seaborne assault against Java also failed. He tried twice to conquer Japan, first in 1274 and again in 1281, when he sent a massive expedition of 4,500 ships and 140,000 men across the

A tiger threatens the heroine in this illustration from a later era portraying a scene in the Yuan dynasty play, *The Disused Kiln,* which tells of a pair of runaway lovers forced to take shelter in an abandoned kiln. Such plays included love stories, comedies, tragedies, and courtroom dramas, and the lines were half-sung and half-spoken.

This impish model of a whistling actor evokes the lively form of drama that originated under the Song and achieved great popularity during the Yuan dynasty, diverting audiences in cities and in the countryside alike.

Sea of Japan. On that occasion, as before, his forces succeeded in landing on the main island, only to be routed by typhoons that shattered his ships and resulted in the loss of nearly half his men.

When Khubilai died in 1294, he left behind a crumbling empire. Neither he nor his Yuan successors ever mastered the art of governing those they conquered. In effect, they were still ruling from horseback—and trampling those whose labor and talents the future of their dynasty depended on.

Through the long bleak years of Mongol occupation, Chinese scholars and artists kept largely to themselves and tended the home fires of their ancestral culture. Particularly in the south, where men of learning had proud memories of public service under the Song, scholars detested the Mongols for destroying their way of life and derided them as unwashed barbarians.

Some educated Chinese toiled as lowly government clerks, but most withdrew from public life and lived as recluses on their estates, entered Buddhist or Daoist monasteries, or taught in private academies. Gone were the days when literati dominated the court and banquet halls. "All the poets have vanished," lamented one writer who visited the old Song capital of Hangzhou after the Mongols took over. He likened himself to "a horse that strolls back and forth, neighing mournfully, when passing by its old stable."

Yet other kinds of artistry flourished in public. Some poets and writers applied their talents to a popular form of musical theater that had sprouted up in northern China before the Mongols arrived. The plots were

sketchy and melodramatic and the stage sets were spare, but the actors compensated by wearing gaudy costumes and offering rousing performances that combined dialogue, song, dance, pantomime, and acrobatics. Gifted authors composed scripts with clever lines and lyrics, and Khubilai himself not only tolerated the shows but patronized them, finding much to enjoy even if he did not understand a good deal of what was being said. Some cities boasted theater districts with dozens of troupes, and traveling companies—often members of a single family—took the shows into the countryside.

Painting enjoyed a renaissance as well. One reason was that artists had more time to practice their craft, since few now held public office. Another was that painting provided a subtle and safe means of protest. One southern artist depicted an orchid without earth around its roots; the earth, he explained discreetly, had been stolen by the barbarians. A reclusive group known as the Eight Talents of Wuxing painted in archaic styles to express their longing for the past and their rejection of the present.

But one young member of that circle, Zhao Mengfu, parted company with his colleagues and moved in a new direction. A

A scholar reclines before a screen, which itself depicts a man of learning seated in front of a screen. Under the Mongols, many Chinese scholars turned inward and quietly devoted themselves to painting, poetry, and scholarship, striving to nurture their culture and protect it from outside influences.

distant relative of the Song imperial family, he was famous enough to be sought after by the Mongols, who coveted the services of eminent Chinese to render their largely foreign administration more acceptable to the populace. Zhao allowed himself to be recruited by the Yuan dynasty in 1286, when he was 32 years old. Appointed to a post in the war ministry in Beijing, he traveled widely, rediscovering the work of old northern masters and winning recognition as a master himself with a style that made fresh use of traditional elements.

The dilemma of "whether to come forth and serve, or to retire in withdrawal," as Zhao put it, tormented others like him who were sought as prize converts to the new regime. Those who yielded and held office rationalized that their presence in the government enabled them to uphold Confucian values and soften Mongol rule. Over time, even some of the fiercest foes of the regime relented a bit. One former Song official resolutely refused to leave his home for 36 years after the conquest, but permitted his sons to serve under the Mongols.

Perhaps the best-known holdout was Wang Yinglin, one of the few men of his age to be recognized as an Erudite, the highest scholarly rank in China. As a prominent Southern Song official, he had written imperial edicts referring to the Mongol invaders as "pigs, swine, and snakes," even as they approached Hangzhou. A maverick and gadfly by nature, he also quarreled with his colleagues and left the court in disgust before the capital fell, retiring to his provincial home, where he devoted himself to scholarship and taught the Confucian classics.

Wang the Erudite would have made a fine showpiece for the Mongols, but he avoided them for nearly two decades. Then around the time of Khubilai's death in 1294, he began accepting government commissions to compose documents commemorating important events in recent Chinese history. Although this meant recognizing the alien rulers he had long shunned, the old scholar evidently harbored little guilt. Like many of his colleagues, he was now confident that the Mongol intrusion was a mere moment in China's long history and that his ancestral culture would endure and ultimately triumph.

That redemption would not be long in coming. In 1368 a new Chinese dynasty, the Ming, would seize power after a lengthy rebellion against the bankrupt Yuan regime and chase the Mongols back onto the steppes. One achievement in particular would come to epitomize the Ming and the lessons they drew from the past—the Great Wall they erected across China's northern frontier, a magnificent if ultimately unsuccessful attempt to keep hostile forces from ever again descending on this land of eternal promise.

# The Three Perfections

"Writing and painting have different names," wrote a ninth-century Chinese art historian, "but a common body." Indeed, Chinese painting, poetry, and calligraphy have long been inextricably linked. At first, the writing that accompanied paintings was done on sheets attached to the pictures. But beginning in the Tang dynasty (AD 618-906), the works of art were inscribed with the poems, and rendered in a flawless hand—a union of "three perfections," as one Chinese emperor put it.

For this marriage of words and images, painters and poets shared the same tools and materials—brushes, inks, and a silk or paper surface. The techniques were similar as well, with the brush strokes used to create the poem resembling those in the painting, yielding a seamless work of art.

The combining of the three perfections usually took place on an evocative landscape painting, with the poem inscribed along one side. The painting sometimes came first, with the artist or the artist's friends contributing the poem. The verse might also have originated with a famous calligrapher, poet, or scholar, or even an emperor or his imperial consort. Such inscriptions could range from abstract verse to complimentary remarks about the artist and the work, and how the writer came to know them.

Other times, the poem itself may have come first, inspiring the artist to paint. Northern Song emperor Huizong regularly held painting competitions based on a line or two of poetry; the paintings would be judged according to how subtly the artist responded to the imagery. In one instance, the emperor assigned the verse: "The horses' hooves were fragrant on returning from trampling flowers." The winning painting depicted butterflies, attracted by the fragrance, fluttering behind the horses.

Emperor Huizong probably inscribed this poem, translated at right, on his painting of birds in a plum tree. The emperor invented this elegant style of calligraphy, which he called "slender gold" for its delicate brushwork and sparing use of ink.

*"Mountain birds, proud and unfettered, Plum blossom pollen, soft and light, This painting will be our covenant, Until a thousand autumns show upon our hoary heads."*

柳陰高士寫高
高枝浪那嚴意
自豪故阅伊人
句絲氏於唐爲
李晉丙询
丁亥春月治题

With a blank scroll before him and an empty wine bowl at his feet, an intoxicated poet-calligrapher sits beneath a willow tree, waiting for inspiration. This painting, by an unknown 11th-century artist, may portray the early scholar Tao Yuanming, who abandoned a government job for a simpler life in the country and the romantic ideal of the artist-recluse.

*"Fearing that in the depth of night the blossoms will sleep and fall, He had tall candles lit to shine on their scarlet finery."*

In Ma Lin's *Waiting for Guests by Candlelight (left)*, a wealthy man sits in his garden pavilion at dusk, basking in the ephemeral beauty of his flowering trees. Servants stand ready to light the candles lining the walkway to illuminate the blossoms in the waning light.

*On a Mountain Path in Spring (right)*, by Song artist Ma Yuan, depicts a scholar strolling beneath a willow tree and gazing into the distance. The painting's poem, translated above right, was inscribed by Lady Yang, consort of Emperor Ningzong (1195-1224) and a noted calligrapher.

# FINDING POETRY IN NATURE

During the Song and Yuan dynasties, poets and painters often retreated from urban life to draw inspiration from nature, where they found a spiritual tranquillity that they tried to convey in their work.

"Looking at a certain painting puts you in a certain mood, as if you were actually there in those mountains," wrote Guo Xi, a master landscape painter of the 11th century. "You see a white path and think you are traveling it. You see the sunset over a level stream and think you are viewing it. . . . You see the cliffside cave, the stones of a spring and think you are roaming there. . . . This is the magic of a painting beyond the mood it imparts."

But magic was not all that was sought by artists such as Guo Xi, for whom there was a moral imperative as well. "What is the purpose of . . . enjoying the landscape?" he asked. "The cultivation of the self amid hills and gardens should be a constant preoccupation."

*"Brushed by his sleeves, wild flowers dance in the wind; Fleeing from him, the hidden birds cut short their song."*

Silhouetted majestically against the skyline, a mountain range dominates this painting by artist Qu Ding. Half-hidden in the panorama are temples, streams, waterfalls, bridges, boats, and travelers. The inscription (translated in part at right) was added in the 18th century by the emperor Qianlong, who counted the work among his collection.

古秀芸峯歲月
多鎬題弥重呼
宣和印看興物
開生面渾是訛
池寫堂窠奴滿
夏山帶暑翠欲
嘗晴峽漸煙波
高樓百尺軒而
做試一憑欄快
若何
戊辰新正月
御題

"The bright valley is about to sing as the waves increase
There is a hundred-foot high tower with open space before us
Just try to lean against the fence and how happy I will be.
Composed by the emperor in the first month
of the lunar year of Wu Chen."

131

"The path [penetrates] deeply to the rustic thatched hut,
Where a tree leans obliquely against the setting sun.
I travel all over the blue mountain paths;
What hill cannot serve as one's home?"

A painting from Wu Zhen's album, called the *Manual of Ink-Bamboo*, portrays the plant's strength and flexibility—qualities valuable to people under foreign occupation. Sprigs of bamboo embrace the poem, which is translated at left.

# ART AS PROTEST

Poets often commented on social issues, and under the Mongols their work was scrutinized by government censors for any hint of treason. Authors dared make only oblique references to their true feelings, and sometimes turned to painting, which became known as *wusheng shi,* or silent poetry.

By creating visual metaphors, the artists could still make their feelings known. For example, artist Wu Zhen chose bamboo, a plant that will bend under heavy snow and will spring back when the snow melts, as the theme of an album of 20 paintings he finished in 1350. In one of the paintings, a snow-laden branch frames a poem that refers to two Chinese heroes from an earlier age, Dong Xuan and Yan Yan, who chose death rather than dishonor:

High principle of Dong Xuan,
Chastity of Yan Yan.
Unbending [even] at the head-chopper,
Stiff-necked against the wind and snow.

The names of these heroes would not have been familiar to the Mongols, but the Chinese who viewed it would have recognized it as a tribute to moral integrity.

*"In the eighth month the Mongol hawk flies low over the ground; In a flurry [the thrush] takes refuge under a tree. The beautiful little bird knows in advance to hide itself; How much more should people act according to circumstances."*

A hawk pursues a thrush in this 14th-century scroll by artist Wang Yuan. The thrush's ability to elude a predator depends on cunning and camouflage, much like the Chinese scholars who tried to keep their jobs without compromising their honor. The Mongol rulers, fond of hunting, may have missed the political implications in this painting. The inscription, added later, is translated below left.

133

# GLOSSARY

**Acupuncture:** an ancient medical treatment, in which long, thin, sharp metal needles are inserted into the body at specific points to relieve pain or cure ailments.

**Adepts:** a term used to refer to devotees of various Daoist practices.

**Advanced scholar:** name given to one who passed the national examination and held the highest and most prestigious degree conferred by the system. Also called a "presented scholar," or *jinshi*.

**Amulet:** a charm, usually worn around the neck, to ward off evil spirits, injury, or misfortune.

**Ancestor worship:** an important system promoting Chinese family unity that is based upon the belief that the spiritual soul will survive as long as it is remembered and honored.

**Bathing the infant:** euphemism for infanticide, a common practice in rural China.

**Battens:** flexible strips of bamboo placed in horizontal pockets along the edge of a junk's sail to stiffen it and keep it flat.

**Block printing:** the earliest known relief-printing method, invented in ninth-century China, utilizing woodcuts to create a design that is subsequently printed on paper by a press or rubbing by hand. Also called woodblock printing.

**Bodhisattva:** in Buddhism, an enlightened being who can become a Buddha but who chooses to remain in the world, forgoing Nirvana, to lead others to salvation.

**Bondage:** serfdom, slavery. In China, a condition entered into by selling oneself or one's children to another.

**Bow:** the front part of a ship.

**Brazier:** a metal pan or container to hold fire or burning coals.

**Buddha:** Siddhartha Gautama of India, the founder of Buddhism; a person who has become Enlightened through living many lifetimes of moral and spiritual development and whose soul, upon death, will escape the transmigration cycle and enter into the eternal state of Nirvana.

**Buddhism:** one of the three major religions of China, introduced there from India in the first century AD; its goal is to obtain spiritual perfection (Enlightenment).

**Bulkhead:** on ships, any of the several separate compartments in the hold that add structural rigidity and prevent a leak from spreading to the entire ship.

**Bureau of Beautiful People:** in Hangzhou's organized underworld, women who specialized in fleecing rich young men.

**Calligraphy:** the art of beautiful handwriting; in China, one of the Three Perfections, often combined with art and poetry to create decorative scrolls.

**Censor:** in imperial China, a government official, working for the Censorate and having direct access to the emperor, whose duty it was to investigate corruption, oppression, subversion, injustice, or mistakes by government employees.

**Chan:** a school of Buddhist thinking (known as Zen in Japan) that held that Enlightenment is potentially available to anyone but could be achieved only by sudden revelation following prolonged isolation from the world and meditation.

**Concubine:** a secondary wife, with lower social status and fewer rights than the primary wife or wives.

**Confucianism:** the most important and influential philosophy and religion of China; based on the teachings of Confucius, it emphasizes the perfectibility of all persons and stresses the concepts of virtue, human kindness, moral achievement, excellence in character, propriety, filial piety, justice, and fidelity to one's true nature.

**Conscript:** one forced by the government to serve in the military; a draftee.

**Consorts:** an emperor's female companions, also called secondary wives or concubines.

**Courtesan:** an exclusive, high-class prostitute, usually trained in the arts, music, and the social graces, whose clients were men of rank or wealth.

**Cutpurse:** a pickpocket.

**Dao (Tao):** literally, the Way, believed by its adherents to be the total, natural, spontaneous, and eternal source of the universe and the governor of all existence.

**Daoism (Taoism):** the mystical philosophy and religion expressed by the legendary writers Laozi and Zhuangzi, based on searching for harmony with the Dao and incorporating within its doctrine ancient beliefs in ghosts, spirits, celestial gods, mythical immortals, and demons; one of the most important and influential belief systems governing Chinese behavior and thought.

**Dharma:** in the Buddhist and Hindu traditions, a law or principle that governs the universe; also, one's conduct in conforming to said law or principle.

**Dowry:** the money, goods, or estate brought by a bride to her husband upon marriage.

**Dragon:** a mythical creature, usually depicted as a huge beast with a serpentine body, the scales of a fish, the ears of an ox, the horns of a stag, the paws of a tiger, and a barbed tail; in China, considered to be a beneficial creature representing yang; from ancient times the symbol of the Chinese emperor.

**Dragon boat:** a long, slender boat with a high bow shaped like a dragon's head and neck and a high stern shaped like a dragon's tail, propelled by 12 or more oarsmen.

**Dynasty:** a hereditary ruling house or family.

**Emperor:** the supreme ruler of an empire; in China, also called the Son of Heaven.

**Empire:** a political entity covering an extensive geographic area and usually having a number of different territories and a variety of peoples with differing languages and cultures under its rule.

**Empress:** the consort or primary wife of an emperor.

**Empress dowager (empress regent):** in imperial China, the mother or paternal grandmother of a young emperor who acted as sovereign and ruled the empire in his stead until he was considered mature enough to rule.

**Erudite:** the highest scholarly rank in China.

**Eunuchs:** castrated men; in China, they were originally responsible for guarding and administering the emperor's harem but in some dynasties became high-ranking government officials with enormous power.

**Ewer:** a widemouthed jug or pitcher, especially a decorative one with an oval body and flaring spout for pouring.

**Exorcism:** a ritual performed by a spirit medium or priest to drive out evil spirits or demons.

**Face diviner:** one who tells a client's fortune by reading the shape of his face; a physiognomist.

**Feet:** on caps, the bamboo- or wire-stiffened sidepieces that were straight, curved, or crossed, depending upon the wearer's status.

**Filial piety:** the most important of the Confucian virtues, the basis of both individual moral conduct and social-political harmony and stability, demonstrated by showing obedience, respect, and devotion towards one's parents and grandparents, putting loyalty to these elders before all else.

**Fire watch:** in Hangzhou, an organized fire patrol posted in observation towers, using flags by day and lanterns by night to direct firefighting squads to blazes in the city.

**Flowers:** name given to the lowest type of prostitutes, who plied their trade on the streets and in shopping arcades.

**Flying tiger warships:** a type of warship propelled by one or more hidden paddle wheels.

**Foot-binding:** the practice of binding the feet of young girls in cloth to make the foot smaller and more appealing, resulting in a deformed foot about three inches long, with a broken arch and toes curled under; outlawed in 1949.

**Gambling Chest:** the card sharks' organization in the Hangzhou underworld.

**Grand Canal:** originally, a series of canals used primarily for transportation but also for irrigation, eventually unified into a single 1,000-mile-long system linking northern and southern China.

**Grand Council:** an advisory panel to the emperor made up of the heads of the Department of State Affairs, the Secretariat, and the Chancellery; the council met daily with the emperor.

**Great Khan:** name given to the supreme ruler of the Mongol Empire who, in actuality, shared his power with the lesser khans that ruled outlying areas.

**Great Principle (the):** under Chinggis Khan, the principle that a soldier either displayed unswerving loyalty to Chinggis and the Mongols or died.

**Great Wall:** an approximately 4,000-mile-long barrier running east to west across China with high defensive masonry and earth walls punctuated periodically by watchtowers; built during the Ming dynasty (AD 1368-1644) to protect China's northern frontier.

**Green Sprouts Act:** a national rural aid program; the act provided farmers with funds from the government for seed in the spring at interest rates lower than those offered by private lenders, with repayment due after the harvest.

**Guilds:** semiofficial merchants' organizations that collected government fees and taxes from their members, regulated trade and transportation of certain commodities, and controlled access to jobs within their given territory or sphere of interest.

**Gurkhan:** literally, "universal ruler." The name given by the Mongols to Chinggis Khan.

**Guru:** a spiritual teacher or guide.

**Harem:** a dwelling or portion of a palace used to house a man's concubines or secondary wives; another name for a group of concubines.

**Headman:** under the Chinese militia system, the man who headed a group of families in the local militia unit and who served as the community chief of police.

**Hemp:** a tall, weedy plant cultivated for its fibers, which were used in making rope and cloth.

**Hitting the cup:** the practice of patronizing small retail wine shops and drinking only one cup of wine.

**Hungry ghosts:** name given to ancestors who, if their souls were not properly honored and propitiated with offerings and rituals, became wandering ghosts, frightening people, scavenging in graveyards, and injuring the living to call attention to their needs.

**Incense burner:** a container with a pierced lid, generally of bronze or pottery, in which incense was burned.

**Ink stone:** a stone with a shallow recess in which pine soot, glue, and water were rubbed to produce the ink used by a calligrapher.

**Jin dynasty** (1115-1234): dynastic name taken by the Jurchens.

**Jinshi:** literally, "advanced scholar," or "presented scholar." Name given to one who passed the national examination and held the highest and most prestigious degree conferred by the system.

**Junk:** a large, oceangoing ship with a flat bottom, high stern, watertight bulkheads in the hold, and rectangular, battened sails of cloth and bamboo that were easily trimmed by being contracted like a Venetian blind.

**Jurchens:** hunting and herding tribes from Manchuria who overthrew the Khitans, conquered the Northern Song, and founded the Jin dynasty; they governed northern China from 1115 to 1234 and were eventually overthrown by the Mongols.

**Karma:** in Buddhism, the belief that one's actions, either good or bad, are always repaid with rewards or retribution in this life or in subsequent incarnations and that most actions, therefore, affect the future course of one's existence.

**Khan:** in China, a ruler of one of three lesser, distant areas of the Mongol Empire called khanates.

**Khitans:** Mongolian-speaking, semiagricultural, seminomadic tribes from Manchuria; as the Liao dynasty, they ruled Manchuria, much of Mongolia, and northern China from the 10th century through the early 12th century, when the dynasty was overthrown by the Jurchens.

**Kowtow:** literally, "knock the head." In China, to show respect and reverence to one's superiors, elders, or venerated objects by kneeling before the person or object and hitting one's forehead against the ground one or more times.

**Lacquer:** a clear or colored coating, made from the sap of the lacquer tree, used to give a high gloss to the surface of an object.

**Lama:** in Tibet, the name by which a Buddhist monk is called.

**Lunisolar:** a calendar system in which the months are lunar (29-30 days, based on the phases of the moon) but the years are solar (based on the course of the sun and the yearly solstices and equinoxes).

**Luohan:** in Buddhism, a person who has attained spiritual perfection and achieved Nirvana; also, a group of divine beings, close disciples of the Buddha, who, although spiritually enlightened and qualified to enter Nirvana, remain in the world to provide people with objects of worship and will not enter Nirvana until the coming of the next Buddha.

**Lychee:** a tree, native to southern China, with small, red, edible fruit about one inch in diameter.

**Magistrate:** in the Chinese civil service system, an official who administered the affairs of a district or county, the lowest unit of government staffed by members of the national government.

**Matchmaker:** one who arranges marriages.

**Middle Kingdom:** name used for the provinces of China or for the Chinese empire as a whole.

**Midwife:** a person, usually a woman, who assists women in childbirth.

**Ming dynasty** (1368-1644): Chinese dynasty noted for achievements in the arts, education, and foreign trade; its first emperor came to power after overthrowing the Yuan dynasty.

**Mongols:** any of a group of primarily nomadic herding and hunting tribes from the steppes of central Asia that were united under Chinggis Khan; they conquered the Jin dynasty and the Southern Song and established the Yuan dynasty, which collapsed in 1368. Although driven back to the steppes, they remained a threat to China until the 17th century, when they were defeated by the Manchus.

**Movable type:** printing technique invented in China during the 11th century in which single characters made of wood, baked clay, tin, or lead were arranged on an iron frame for printing, then removed and reused.

**Moxibustion:** an ancient Chinese medical treatment in which heat, in the form of hot rods or burning herbs, was applied to specific parts of the body to treat diseases and reduce pain.

**Muslim:** one who follows the teachings of Muhammad; an adherent of the Islamic faith.

**Neo-Confucianism:** a reinterpretation of classical Confucianism, incorporating some ideas and concepts from Daoism and Buddhism; the form of Confucianism dominant from the Song dynasty to the 20th century.

**Neo-Confucianists:** a group of Chinese scholars and scholar-officials, led by the philosopher Zhu Xi, who rediscovered, reinterpreted, and practiced the philosophical principles of the Confucian classics, incorporating some ideas and concepts from Daoism and Buddhism in the process.

**Nepotism:** bestowing favors upon one's relatives or friends, particularly in business dealings or employment.

**New Policies:** a series of highly controversial reforms enacted in 1069 to strengthen the state and improve the lives of the peasants. The reforms drew strong opposition from rich landowners and scholar-officials.

**New Year's Day:** one of the primary celebrations of the Chinese year, coinciding with the second new moon after the winter solstice and falling between January 21 and February 16.

**Night soil:** euphemism for a city's human excrement, collected during the night and sold as fertilizer in the suburbs.

**Noble Consort:** name given to an emperor's highest ranking consort.

**Paddy:** a small, level field in which rice is grown; using a system of dams, dikes, and sluice gates to control the water level, it is flooded for three-fourths of the growing season to a depth of four to six inches but drained for the harvest.

**Palanquin:** a covered litter (portable bed or couch), usually for one person, carried on poles on the shoulders of two or four men or, if very large, by animals.

**Pharmacopoeia:** a list of medicinal agents (generally herbs and minerals), often including information necessary for their preparation and use.

**Phoenix:** a large mythical bird dwelling in the south, originally the symbol of fire but later the symbol of the empress, often used as a decorative design on artwork and other objects.

**Physiognomist:** a face diviner, one who read a client's fortune by analyzing the shape of the person's face.

**Polder:** a low-lying tract of land reclaimed from a body of water and protected from its encroachment by dikes.

**Pouring man:** one who collected and carted away a city's excrement each night, selling it as fertilizer for gardens in the suburbs.

**Prefect:** an administrative official of a prefecture, a position several grades above the magistrate of a county.

**Protection:** a privilege that allowed a high official to place younger male relatives in the bureaucracy without their having to take an examination.

**Pure Land:** a Buddhist sect that believed that the Buddha presided over paradise and offered salvation to all who invoked his name.

**Rabbit horses:** small packhorses approximately three feet high.

**Regent:** an individual who ruled during the minority or incapacitation of an emperor.

**Rice paddy:** another name for a paddy.

**Sage:** in Confucianism, a person who has perfected himself to such a degree that he has penetrated the Way and understands the principles of Heaven and Earth.

**Scholar-official:** a man who had passed the national examination; the highest social class in China, with enormous political power, its members were often close advisers to the emperor.

**Scholar's cap:** a type of cap with sidepieces (feet) extending horizontally from the cap itself, worn only by the emperor and his leading officials.

**Scribes:** in China, calligraphers who were employed by official bureaus or who plied their trade on the streets.

**Scroll painting:** a painting, frequently embellished with calligraphy and poetry, created on a continuous roll of paper or silk.

**Sculling oar:** one of a pair of oars, usually less than 10 feet long, used by one person at the stern of a boat to propel the vessel.

**Secondary wife:** any wife other than the primary wife, with lower social status and fewer rights than the primary wife; concubine.

**Sedan chair:** a portable enclosed chair for one person, mounted on long, horizontal parallel poles and carried by two men.

**Siege warfare:** a prolonged military action in which an army surrounds and blockades a city, town, or fortress and attempts to breach its fortifications, meanwhile cutting off the residents' supply of food and/or water from the outside.

**Slender gold:** a particularly elegant style of calligraphy, so called for its delicate brushwork and sparing use of ink.

**Song dynasty** (960-1279): Chinese ruling dynasty founded by Zhao Kuangyin and noted for enormous economic development as well as the magnificent artistic achievements of the period. After 1126, when the dynasty lost its northern territory to the Jurchens, the Song dynasty ruled only in southern China and is known as the Southern Song.

**Son of Heaven:** name given to the emperors of China, who were seen as descendants of heaven with the ability to act as intermediaries between the people on earth and the spirits on high.

**Southern Song** (1126-1279): name given to the Song dynasty after its expulsion from northern China and re-establishment in southern China; conquered in 1279 by the Mongols.

**Star gods:** in Chinese mythology, any of the three stellar gods, called Fu-Shou-Lu.

**Steppe:** a vast, semiarid, grassy, generally treeless, plain extending approximately 4,000 miles across Asia from modern-day Romania eastward to Manchuria and varying from 200 to 600 miles from north to south.

**Stern:** the rear part of a ship or boat.

**Sumptuary laws:** laws designed to regulate the ownership and use of luxury goods, intended to restrict the finest possessions to those of highest rank.

**Supreme Commander of the Palace:** the matron in charge of the six bureaus of female retainers that served the emperor and his retinue and generally operated the imperial palace.

**Talented One:** name given to the lowest ranking of an emperor's consorts.

**Talisman:** an amulet or charm carved with one or more magical signs and figures, worn to afford its owner the protection of the star gods, avert evil, and bring good fortune; an object used by a Daoist priest in curing illnesses.

**Tanguts:** a Tibetan tribal people, the first group conquered by Chinggis Khan prior to his march on China. Also known as the Hsi Hsia.

**Tao:** a commonly encountered alternate spelling of Dao.

**Three Perfections:** calligraphy, poetry, and painting, often combined to create delicate scenes graced with beautifully inscribed lines of verse on scrolls.

**Water taxi:** a passenger-carrying boat available for hire.

**Way (the):** Dao, believed by Daoists to be the total, natural, spontaneous, and eternal source of the universe and the governor of all existence.

**Wok:** a thin-walled metal pan with a rounded bottom and sloping sides used in stir-frying and steaming foods; the Cantonese pronunciation of the Mandarin word guo, or pot.

**Woodblock printing:** the earliest known relief-printing method, invented in ninth-century China, utilizing woodcuts to create a design subsequently printed on paper. Also called block printing.

**Woodcut:** an engraving on a block of wood used in printing, also called a woodblock; a print made from such an engraving.

**Wusheng shi:** silent poetry; a form of expression used by Chinese poets during the years of Mongol domination in which the poets painted or wrote about social issues in such a way that government censors, who were usually not native Chinese, could not understand the true meaning of the work.

**Xiao:** literally, "filial piety," the most important of the Confucian virtues, displayed by showing obedience, respect, and devotion toward one's parents and grandparents (or in the case of a woman, those of her husband), putting loyalty to these elders before all else.

**Yin/Yang:** in Chinese dualistic philosophy, the two complementary aspects, or positive and negative influences, that permeate all matter and aspects of life, with yin representing the passive, female aspect and yang the active, male aspect.

**Yuan dynasty** (1206-1368): name taken officially in 1271 by the Mongol dynasty founded in 1206 by Chinggis Khan.

**Zhong Kui:** a mythical demon queller.

# PRONUNCIATION GUIDE

Aguda (ah-gu-dah)
Ahmad (AH-mahd)
Amitabha (ah-mee-TAH-bah)
Arigh Böke (ah-reek beu-keh)
Bakhtakh (bahk-tahk)
Beijing (bay-jing)
Bing (bing)
Bi Sheng (bee shuhng)
Bodhisattva (bo-dee-SAHT-vah)
Buddha (BOO-dah)
Cao (tsow)
Chabi (chah-bee)
Chan (chahn)
Changzhou (chahng-joe)
Chinggis Khan (CHING-gis kahn)
Dao (dow)
Dao de jing (dow duhh jing)
Dong Xuan (doong shwen)
Dorji (dor-jee)
Duzong (doo-dzoong)
Fei (fay)
Fuzhou (foo-joe)
Gaozong (gow-dzoong)
Geisha (GAY-shah)
Gongdi (goong-dee)
Guo Xi (gwohh shee)
Gurkhan (GUR-kahn)
Güyüg (GEU-yeuk)
Hainan (hai-nahn)
Hangzhou (hahng-joe)
Henan (huhh-nahn)
Huai (hwy)
Huanghe (hwahng-huhh)
Huizhou (hwey-joe)
Huzhou (hoo-joe)
Huizong (hwey-dzoong)
Jiangxi (jyahng-shee)
Jia Sidao (jyah ss-dow)
Jin (jin)
Jinshi (jin-shur)
Jurchens (jer-chehns)

Kaifeng (kai-fuhng)
Khaidu (KAI-du)
Khan (kahn)
Khitan (kee-tahn)
Khubilai (KOO-bee-lai)
Kongzi (koong-dzuh)
Laozi (lau-dzuh)
Liao (lyow)
Liao Yingzhong (lyow ying-dzoong)
Liu (lyoe)
Liu Bingzhong (lyoe bing-joong)
Lizong (lee-dzoong)
Luohan (lwohh-hahn)
Lychee (lee-chee)
Ma Lin (mah lin)
Ma Yuan (mah ywen)
Meng (muhng)
Ming (ming)
Mizhou (mee-joe)
Möngke (MEUNG-keh)
Nanjing (nahn-jing)
Nayan (nai-yahn)
Ningzong (ning-dzoong)
Ögödei (EU-geu-day)
Pingjiang (ping-jyahng)
Qianlong (chyen-loong)
Qinzong (chin-dzoong)
Qu Ding (chyew ding)
Renzong (run-dzoong)
Shandong (shahn-doong)
Shangdu (shahng-doo)
Shenzong (shun-dzoong)
Shi (shur)
Sichuan (ss-chwahn)
Siddhartha Gautama (sid-dar-tah gow-tah-mah)
Sima Guang (ss-mah gwahng)
Song (soong)
Sorghaghtani Beki (SOR-gahg-tah-nee beh-kee)
Su Che (soo chuh)
Su Dongpo (soo doong-pwohh)
Su Shi (soo shur)

Su Song (soo soong)
Suzhou (soo-joe)
Taizong (tai-dzoong)
Taizu (tai-dzoo)
Tang (tahng)
Tanguts (tahng-oots)
Tao Yuanming (tao ywen-ming)
Tolui (TOE-loo-ee)
Wang Anshi (wahng ahn-shur)
Wang Chen (wahng chuhn)
Wang Ge (wahng guhh)
Wang Yinglin (wahng ying-lin)
Wang Yuan (wahng ywen)
Wen Tianxiang (wen tyen-shyahng)
Wusheng shi (woo-shung shur)
Wuxing (woo-shing)
Wu Zhen (woo jen)
Xiao (shyow)
Xie (shyeh)
Xie Qiao (shyeh chyow)
Yaishan (yai-shahn)
Yan Yan (yen yen)
Yang (yahng)
Yangzi (yahng-dzih)
Yelü Chucai (yeh-leu choo-tsai)
Yingzong (ying-dzoong)
Yuan (ywen)
Zhang Zu (jahng dzoo)
Zhao (jow)
Zhao Kuangyin (jow kwahng-yin)
Zhao Mengfu (jow muhng-foo)
Zhe (juhh)
Zheng (juhng)
Zhezong (juhh-dzoong)
Zhongdu (joong-doo)
Zhou (joe)
Zongdu (dzoong-doo)
Zhu (joo)
Zhuangzi (jwahng-dzuh)
Zhu Xi (joo shee)
Zhu Yuanzhang (joo ywen-jahng)

# ACKNOWLEDGMENTS AND PICTURE CREDITS

**ACKNOWLEDGMENTS**

The editors wish to thank the following individuals and institutions for their valuable assistance in the preparation of this volume:
Tony Chen, National Palace Museum, Taipei; Sybille Giermond, Museum für Ostasiatische Kunst, Köln; Guo Baoqi, *Time* Magazine, Beijing; Heidrun Klein, Bildarchiv Preussischer Kulturbesitz, Berlin; Ingo Nentwig, Museum für Völkerkunde zu Leipzig, Leipzig; Scott A. Thompson, the Freer Gallery of Art, Washington, D.C.; Xia Jingping, Palace Museum, Beijing.

# BIBLIOGRAPHY
## BOOKS

Anderson, E. N. *The Food of China.* New Haven, Conn.: Yale University Press, 1988.

Baoqun, Luan, comp. *Tales about Chinese Emperors* (2d ed.). Ed. and trans. by Tang Bowen. Hong Kong: Hai Feng, 1995.

Blunden, Caroline, and Mark Elvin. *Cultural Atlas of China.* New York: Facts On File, 1983.

*Body, Subject & Power in China.* Ed. by Angela Zito and Tani E. Barlow. Chicago: University of Chicago Press, 1994.

Buchanan, Keith, Charles P. FitzGerald, and Colin A. Ronan. *China.* New York: Crown, 1981.

Burton, John A. *Animals of the World: A Guide to More Than 300 Mammals.* Philadelphia: Running Press, 1994.

Cahill, James. *The Painter's Practice: How Artists Lived and Worked in Traditional China.* New York: Columbia University Press, 1994.

*The Cambridge Encyclopedia of China* (2d ed.). Cambridge: Cambridge University Press, 1991.

*The Cambridge History of China, Vol. 1: The Ch'in and Han Empires, 221 B.C.-A.D. 220.* Ed. by Denis Twitchett and Michael Loewe. Cambridge: Cambridge University Press, 1986.

Canby, Courtlandt. *A History of Ships and Seafaring* (Vol. 2). New York: Hawthorn Books, 1963.

Casson, Lionel. *Illustrated History of Ships & Boats.* Garden City, N.Y.: Doubleday, 1964.

Chaffee, John W. *The Thorny Gates of Learning in Sung China.* Cambridge: Cambridge University Press, 1985.

Chang, K. C., ed. *Food in Chinese Culture: Anthropological and Historical Perspectives.* New Haven, Conn.: Yale University Press, 1977.

*China: Ancient Culture, Modern Land.* Norman: University of Oklahoma Press, 1994.

*China: Eine Weige der Weltkultur.* Mainz, Germany: Verlag Philipp von Zabern, 1994.

*Chinese Herbal Medicine: Materia Medica.* Comp. and trans. by Dan Bensky and Andrew Gamble. Seattle: Eastland Press, 1993.

Christie, Anthony. *Chinese Mythology.* New York: Peter Bedrick Books, 1987.

Chung, Priscilla Ching. *Palace Women in the Northern Sung: 960-1126.* Leiden, Netherlands: E. J. Brill, 1981.

Clayre, Alasdair. *The Heart of the Dragon.* Boston: Houghton Mifflin, 1985.

Clunas, Craig. *Art in China.* Oxford: Oxford University Press, 1997.

Cohen, Misha Ruth. *The Chinese Way to Healing: Many Paths to Wholeness.* New York: A Perigee Book, 1996.

Cotterell, Arthur. *Ancient China.* New York: Alfred A. Knopf, 1994.

Cotterell, Yong Yap, and Arthur Cotterell. *The Early Civilization of China.* London: Weidenfeld and Nicolson, 1975.

Croizier, Ralph C. *Traditional Medicine in Modern China: Science, Nationalism, and the Tensions of Cultural Change.* Cambridge, Mass.: Harvard University Press, 1968.

Davis, Richard L. *Wind against the Mountain: The Crisis of Politics and Culture in Thirteenth-Century China.* Cambridge, Mass.: Harvard University Press, 1996.

Durant, Will. *Our Oriental Heritage* (Vol. 1 of *The Story of Civilization*). New York: Simon and Schuster, 1954.

Egan, Ronald C. *Word, Image, and Deed in the Life of Su Shi.* Cambridge, Mass.: Harvard University Press, 1994.

Eisenberg, David. *Encounters with Qi: Exploring Chinese Medicine.* New York: Penguin Books, 1985.

Elvin, Mark. *The Pattern of the Chinese Past: A Social and Economic Interpretation.* Stanford, Calif.: Stanford University Press, 1973.

Embrey, Patricia Buckley:
*The Cambridge Illustrated History of China.* Cambridge: Cambridge University Press, 1996.
*The Inner Quarters: Marriage and the Lives of Chinese Women in the Sung Period.* Berkeley: University of California Press, 1993.

Embrey, Patricia Buckley, ed. *Chinese Civilization: A Sourcebook.* New York: Free Press, 1993.

Embrey, Patricia Buckley, trans. *Family and Property in Sung China.* Princeton, N.J.: Princeton University Press, 1984.

Embrey, Patricia Buckley, and Peter N. Gregory, eds. *Religion and Society in T'ang and Sung China.* Honolulu: University of Hawaii Press, 1993.

Fitzgerald, C. P.:
*China: A Short Cultural History.* New York: Frederick A. Praeger, 1961.
*The Horizon History of China.* New York: American Heritage, 1969.

Fong, Wen C., and James C. Y. Watt. *Possessing the Past: Treasures from the National Palace Museum, Taipei.* New York: Metropolitan Museum of Art, 1996.

Franke, Herbert. *China under Mongol Rule.* Aldershot, Hampshire, England: Variorum, 1994.

Franke, Herbert, and Denis Twitchett, eds. *The Cambridge History of China, Vol. 6: Alien Regimes and Border States, 907-1368.* Cambridge: Cambridge University Press, 1994.

Gaur, Albertine. *A History of Writing.* New York: Cross River Press, 1992.

Gernet, Jacques:
*Daily Life in China: On the Eve of the Mongol Invasion, 1250-1276.* Trans. by H. M. Wright. New York: Macmillan, 1962.
*History of Chinese Civilization.* Trans. by J. R. Foster. Cambridge: Cambridge University Press, 1982.

Guisso, Richard W., and Stanley Johannesen, eds. *Women in China: Current Directions in Historical Scholarship.* Youngstown, N.Y.: Philo Press, 1981.

Haeger, John Winthrop, ed. *Crisis and Prosperity in Sung China.* Tucson: University of Arizona Press, 1975.

Hansen, Valerie. *Changing Gods in Medieval China, 1127-1276.* Princeton, N.J.: Princeton University Press, 1990.

Hibbert, Christopher. *Cities and Civilizations.* New York: Welcome Rain, 1996.

Hsu, Hong-Yen. *How to Treat Yourself with Chinese Herbs.* New Canaan, Conn.: Keats Publishing, 1980.

Hucker, Charles O. *China's Imperial Past: An Introduction to Chinese History and Culture.* Stanford, Calif.: Stanford University Press, 1975.

Jay, Jennifer W. *A Change in Dynasties: Loyalism in Thirteenth-Century China.* Bellingham, Wash.: Western Washington, 1991.

Kahn, Paul. *The Secret History of the Mongols: The Origin of Chinghis Khan.* San Francisco: North Point Press, 1984.

Kaptchuk, Ted J. *The Web That Has No Weaver: Understanding Chinese Medicine.* Chicago: Congdon & Weed, 1983.

Kerr, Rose, Verity Wilson, and Craig Clunas. *Chinese Art and Design.* Ed. by Rose Kerr. London: Victoria and Albert Museum, 1991.

Keswick, Maggie. *The Chinese Garden: History, Art & Architecture.* New York: Rizzoli, 1978.

Langlois, John D., Jr., ed. *China under Mongol Rule.* Princeton, N.J.: Princeton University Press, 1981.

Latham, Ronald, trans. *The Travels of Marco Polo.* New York: Abaris Books, 1982.

Lee, Sherman E., and Wai-Kam Ho. *Chinese Art under the Mongols: The Yüan Dynasty (1279-1368).* Cleveland: Cleveland Museum of Art, 1968.

Leslie, Charles. *Asian Medical Systems: A Comparative Study.* Berkeley: University of California Press, 1976.

Levy, Howard S. *Chinese Footbinding: The History of a Curious Erotic Custom.* New York: Walter Rawls, 1966.

Li, Zhiyan, and Cheng Wen. *Chinese Pottery and Porcelain.* Beijing: Foreign Languages Press, 1984.

*Light in the East: TimeFrame AD 1000-1100* (Time Frame series). Alexandria, Va.: Time-Life Books, 1988.

Lin, Shuen-Fu. *The Transformation of the Chinese Lyrical Tradition: Chiang K'uei and Southern Sung Tz'u Poetry.* Princeton, N.J.: Princeton University Press, 1978.

Lin, Yutang. *The Gay Genius: The Life and Times of Su Tungpo.* Westport, Conn.: Greenwood Press, 1971.

Lopez, Donald S., Jr., ed. *Religions of China in Practice.* Princeton, N.J.: Princeton University Press, 1996.

McKnight, Brian E. *Law and Order in Sung China.* Cambridge: Cambridge University Press, 1992.

Major, Ralph H. *A History of Medicine* (Vol. 1). Springfield, Ill.: Charles C. Thomas, 1954.

Marshall, Robert. *Storm from the East: From Genghis Khan to Khubilai Khan.* London: BBC Books, 1993.

Martin, H. Desmond. *The Rise of Chingis Khan and His Conquest of North China.* Baltimore: Johns Hopkins Press, 1950.

Merson, John. *The Genius That Was China.* Woodstock, N.Y.: Overlook Press, 1990.

Meskill, John, ed. *An Introduction to Chinese Civilization.* Lexington, Mass.: D. C. Heath, 1973.

*The Mongol Conquests: TimeFrame AD 1200-1300* (Time Frame series). Alexandria, Va.: Time-Life Books, 1989.

Morgan, David. *The Mongols.* Oxford: Basil Blackwell, 1986.

Morris, Edwin T. *The Gardens of China: History, Art, and Meanings.* New York: Charles Scribner's Sons, 1983.

National Palace Museum. *Painting of Children at Play.* Taipei: National Palace Museum, 1990.

Needham, Joseph:
*History of Scientific Thought* (Vol. 2). Cambridge: Cambridge University Press, 1991.
*Mathematics and the Sciences of the Heavens and the Earth* (Vol. 3). Cambridge: Cambridge University Press, 1959.
*Science and Civilisation in China: Introductory Orientations* (Vol. 1). Cambridge: Cambridge University Press, 1965.

*The New Columbia Encyclopedia.* Ed. by William H. Harris and Judith S. Levey. New York: Columbia University Press, 1975.

*Ordering the World.* Ed. by Robert P. Hymes and Conrad Schirokauer. Berkeley: University of California Press, 1993.

Overmyer, Daniel L. *Religions of China: The World as a Living System.* San Francisco: Harper & Row, 1986.

Panati, Charles. *Extraordinary Origins of Everyday Things.* New York: Harper & Row, 1987.

Pien-ch'ueh. *Nan-ching: The Classic of Difficult Issues.* Trans. by Paul U. Unschuld. Berkeley: University of California Press, 1986.

Polo, Marco. *The Description of the World.* London: George Routledge & Sons, 1938.

Rawson, Jessica, et al. *The British Museum Book of Chinese Art.* Ed. by Jessica Rawson. London: British Museum Press, 1992.

Ross, Nancy Wilson. *Three Ways of Asian Wisdom.* New York: Simon & Schuster, 1966.

Rossabi, Morris, ed. *China among Equals.* Berkeley: University of California Press, 1983.

Rugoff, Milton. *Marco Polo's Adventures in China.* New York: American Heritage Publishing, 1964.

Sanders, Tao Tao Liu. *Dragons, Gods & Spirits from Chinese Mythology.* New York: Schocken Books, 1983.

Shang, Xizhi, comp. *Tales of Empresses and Imperial Consorts in China.* Trans. by Sun Haichen. Hong Kong: Hai Feng, 1994.

Sickman, Laurence, and Alexander Soper. *The Art and Architecture of China.* Harmondsworth, Middlesex, England: Penguin Books, 1971.

Smith, Bradley, and Wan-go Weng. *A History in Art.* New York: Doubleday & Co., 1979.

*Splendors of Imperial China: Treasures from the National Palace Museum, Taipei.* New York: Metropolitan Museum of Art, 1996.

*Storm across Asia* (Vol. 7 of *Imperial Visions: The Rise and Fall of Empires* series). New York: HBJ Press, 1980.

Sullivan, Michael:
*The Arts of China.* Berkeley: University of California Press, 1984.
*The Three Perfections: Chinese Painting, Poetry and Calligraphy.* New York: George Braziller, 1980.

Temple, Robert. *The Genius of China: 3,000 Years of Science, Discovery, and Invention.* New York: Simon & Schuster, 1986.

Trubner, Henry, William Jay Rathbun, and Catherine A. Kaputa. *Asiatic Art in the Seattle Art Museum.* Seattle: Seattle Art Museum, 1973.

Unschuld, Paul U. *Medical Ethics in Imperial China.* Berkeley: University of California Press, 1979.

Valenstein, Susanne G. *A Handbook of Chinese Ceramics.* New York: Metropolitan Museum of Art, 1975.

Van Loon, Hendrik Willem. *Ships & How They Sailed the Seven Seas: 5000 B.C.-A.D. 1935.* New York: Simon and Schuster, 1935.

Whitefield, Roderick, and Anne Farrer. *Caves of the Thousand Buddhas: Chinese Art from the Silk Route.* New York: George Braziller, 1990.

Wiencek, Henry. *Genghis Khan and the Mongols.* Glenn D. Lowry. *The Mongul Expansion.* In *Storm across Asia* (*Imperial Visions: The Rise and Fall of Empires* series). New York: HBJ Press, 1980.

Williams, Suzanne. *Made in China: Ideas and Inventions from Ancient China.* Berkeley, Calif.: Pacific View Press, 1996.

Williamson, H. R. *Wang An Shih: A Chinese Statesman and Educationalist of the Sung Dynasty* (Vol. 1). Westport, Conn.: Hyperion Press, 1935.

Wills, John E., Jr. *Mountain of Fame: Portraits in Chinese History.* Princeton, N.J.: Princeton University Press, 1994.

Worcester, G. R. G:
*Junks and Sampans of the Upper Yangtze.* Shanghai: Statistical Dept. of the Inspectorate General of Customs, 1940.
*The Junks & Sampans of the Yangtze.* Annapolis, Md.: Naval Institute Press, 1971.
*Sail and Sweep in China.* London: H.M.S.O., 1966.

*The World of Buddhism: Buddhist Monks and Nuns in Society and Culture.* Ed. by Heinz Bechert and Richard Gombrich. London: Thames and Hudson, 1984.

Wright, Arthur F. *Buddhism in Chinese History.* Stanford, Calif.: Stanford University Press, 1959.

Wright, Arthur F., and Denis Twitchett, eds. *Confucian Personalities.* Stanford, Calif.: Stanford University Press, 1962.

Zhou, Xun, and Gao Chunming. *5000 Years of Chinese Costumes.* Hong Kong: Commercial Press, 1987.

Zhu, Jiajin, comp. *Treasures of the Forbidden City.* New York: Viking, 1986.

## PERIODICALS

Edwards, Mike. "Genghis Khan." *National Geographic,* December 1996.

*Monumenta Serica: Journal of Oriental Studies,* 1988-1989, Vol. 38.

## OTHER SOURCES

The Freer Gallery of Art, comp. *Chinese Calligraphy.* In *The Freer Gallery of Art: China.* Washington, D.C.: Freer Gallery of Art, n.d.

# INDEX

Time-Life Books is a division of Time Life Inc.

**TIME LIFE INC.**
PRESIDENT and CEO: George Artandi

**TIME-LIFE BOOKS**
PRESIDENT: Stephen R. Frary
PUBLISHER/MANAGING EDITOR: Neil Kagan
VICE PRESIDENT, MARKETING: Joseph A. Kuna

*What Life Was Like* ®
**IN THE LAND OF THE DRAGON**

EDITOR: Denise Dersin
DIRECTOR, NEW PRODUCT DEVELOPMENT:
Elizabeth D. Ward
DIRECTOR OF MARKETING:
Pamela R. Farrell

*Deputy Editor:* Marion Ferguson Briggs
*Art Director:* Alan Pitts
*Text Editors:* Stephen G. Hyslop, Jarelle S. Stein
*Associate Editor/Research and Writing:*
Sharon Kurtz Thompson
*Senior Copyeditor:* Mary Beth Oelkers-Keegan
*Technical Art Specialist:* John Drummond
*Picture Coordinator:* David Herod
*Editorial Assistant:* Christine Higgins

*Special Contributors:* Ronald H. Bailey, Susan Perry, Ellen
Phillips (chapter text); Diane Gerard, Christine Hauser,
Donna M. Lucey, Marilyn Murphy Terrell, Elizabeth
Thompson (research-writing); Arlene Borden, Holly
Downen, Beth Levin (research); Janet Cave (editing);
Lina Baber Burton (glossary); Holly Downen (overread);
Barbara L. Klein (index).

*Correspondents:* Maria Vincenza Aloisi (Paris), Christine
Hinze (London), Christina Lieberman (New York).
Valuable assistance was also provided by: Forrest Anderson
(Beijing), Angelika Lemmer (Bonn), Don Shapiro
(Taipei), Hiroko Tashiro (Tokyo).

*Director of Finance:* Christopher Hearing
*Directors of Book Production:* Marjann Caldwell,
Patricia Pascale
*Director of Publishing Technology:* Betsi McGrath
*Director of Photography and Research:* John Conrad Weiser
*Director of Editorial Administration:* Barbara Levitt
*Production Manager:* Gertraude Schaefer
*Quality Assurance Manager:* James King
*Chief Librarian:* Louise D. Forstall

*Consultant:*
Paul Rakita Goldin is assistant professor of Chinese at the
University of Pennsylvania and specializes in traditional
Chinese history and philosophy. He received his under-
graduate degree from the University of Pennsylvania and
his Ph.D. from Harvard University. Professor Goldin is the
author of *The Philosophy of Xunzi,* a study of China's third-
century-BC foundational thinker, in addition to numerous
scholarly articles. His current research focuses on intellectual conceptions of sex and society in ancient China.

**Library of Congress Cataloging-in-Publication Data**
What life was like in the land of the dragon :
imperial China, AD 960-1368 /
by the editors of Time-Life Books.
       p.      cm. (What life was like series)
      Includes bibliographical references and index.
      ISBN 0-7835-5458-3
      1. China—Social life and customs—960-1644.
2. China—History—Sung dynasty, 960-1279. 3. China—
History—Yüan dynasty, 1260-1368.
I. Time-Life Books. II. Series
DS750.72 W46 1998               98-25851
951'.024—dc21                  CIP

*Other Publications:*
HISTORY
The American Story
Voices of the Civil War
The American Indians
Lost Civilizations
Mysteries of the Unknown
Time Frame
The Civil War
Cultural Atlas

COOKING
Weight Watchers® Smart Choice Recipe Collection
Great Taste~Low Fat
Williams-Sonoma Kitchen Library

SCIENCE/NATURE
Voyage Through the Universe

DO IT YOURSELF
The Time-Life Complete Gardener
Home Repair and Improvement
The Art of Woodworking
Fix It Yourself

TIME-LIFE KIDS
Library of First Questions and Answers
A Child's First Library of Learning
I Love Math
Nature Company Discoveries
Understanding Science & Nature

For information on and a full description of any of
the Time-Life Books series listed above, please call
1-800-621-7026 or write:

Reader Information
Time-Life Customer Service
P.O. Box C-32068
Richmond, Virginia 23261-2068

This volume is one in a series on world history that
uses contemporary art, artifacts, and personal accounts to
create an intimate portrait of daily life in the past.

Other volumes included in the
*What Life Was Like* series:

*On the Banks of the Nile: Egypt, 3050-30 BC*
*In the Age of Chivalry: Medieval Europe, AD 800-1500*
*When Rome Ruled the World: The Roman Empire, 100 BC-AD 200*
*At the Dawn of Democracy: Classical Athens, 525-322 BC*
*When Longships Sailed: Vikings, AD 800-1100*
*Among Druids and High Kings: Celtic Ireland, AD 400-1200*
*In the Realm of Elizabeth: England, AD 1533-1603*
*Amid Splendor and Intrigue: Byzantine Empire, AD 330-1453*

951    What life was like in the
WHA       land of the dragon
                                        B

**DATE DUE**

| DEC 16 98 | | | |
|---|---|---|---|
| JAN 04 '99 | | | |
| JAN 22 '99 | | | |
| FEB 04 '99 | | | |
| JUN 08 '99 | | | |
| AUG 04 | | | |
| AUG 25 | | | |
| APR 27 2002 | | | |
| FEB 26 '0 | | | |
| APR 01 0 | | | |
| | | | |
| | | | |

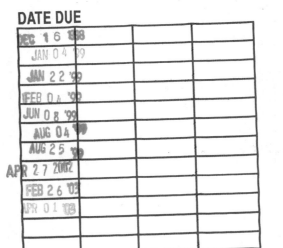

Date _____ Nov 1998 _____

## SEDRO-WOOLLEY PUBLIC LIBRARY
### Sedro-Woolley, WA 98284